American Politics

0 1 1

2

American Politics:

Strategy and Choice

WILLIAM T. BIANCO
PENNSYLVANIA STATE UNIVERSITY

W·W·NORTON & COMPANY
New York • *London*

The text of this book is composed in Galliard
with the display set in Modern 216 Light
Composition by PennSet, Inc.
Manufacturing by The Courier Companies, Inc.
Book design by Jacques Chazaud

Library of Congress Cataloging-in-Publication Data
Bianco, William T., 1960–
    American politics : strategy and choice / William T. Bianco.
      p. cm.
    Includes bibliographical references and index.
    ISBN 0-393-97610-6 (pbk.)
    1. United States—Politics and government. 2. Rational choice theory. I. Title.

  JK271 .B57 2000
  320.973—dc21

                        00–033229

W. W. Norton & Company, Inc., 500 Fifth Avenue, New York, N.Y. 10110
www.wwnorton.com

W. W. Norton & Company Ltd., 10 Coptic Street, London WC1A 1PU

1 2 3 4 5 6 7 8 9 0

For my teachers,
Steve Brown and John Scholz,
Dick Fenno and Bill Riker,
John Aldrich and Bob Bates

Contents

Acknowledgments

More than anything else, this book reflects my experiences with some two thousand students in various incarnations of Intro American Politics. I learned to teach by teaching them. I am also indebted to the legion of teaching assistants who have worked with me over the years, especially Dan Lipinski, Sarah Poggione, Matt Schousen, Danielle Vinson, and Rich Waddell.

My editor, Steve Dunn, has nurtured this project from the beginning. He has been an unflagging source of support, enthusiasm, and advice. Having made it impossible for me to say no, I hope he is pleased with the results.

I have also benefited from reviews by David Canon, Paul Gronke, and John Wilkerson. They are all longtime friends, but as best as I can tell, this fact made little difference. Their reviews were exhaustive, frequently critical, and generally on the mark. This is a much better book for their work. I cannot thank them enough.

As always, my toughest, most insightful, and gentlest critic was Regina Smyth, whose intuitions about teaching are far better than mine.

Finally, writing this book allows me to acknowledge an enormous debt that I owe to the people who taught me. My undergraduate mentors, Steve Brown and John Scholz, were the first to suggest that I think about a career in academia and we spent many hours talking about how to pursue this ambition. In graduate school at the University of Rochester, Dick Fenno and Bill Riker were exemplars of what it meant to be a first-rate scholar, teacher, and colleague. And at my first tenure-track job at Duke University, John Aldrich and Bob Bates demonstrated how much more I had to learn, then volunteered to help finish my education.

In recognition and in gratitude, this book is dedicated to them.

American Politics

1

Introduction

The goal of this book is to convince you that American politics is not as confusing, chaotic, or unexplainable as most people think. The central premise is that nothing in politics happens by accident—everything you see is the result of the choices people make. The focus here is on understanding American politics by examining these choices and their consequences.

The central assumption in this book is that people are rational actors. As it is used here, the term *rational* has a very special and narrow meaning. Simply put, a rational actor always makes decisions that are consistent with his or her goals. One of the primary goals of this book is to show you that many of the seemingly bizarre, random, or otherwise inexplicable features of modern American politics are in fact the product of rational, goal-driven choices.

A good example comes from Chapter Four's analysis of the decision to vote. Even in a close presidential race, like those of 1968 or 1976, only about two-thirds of those eligible to vote actually did so. Why do so many people abstain when they have strong feelings about who should win?

Chapter Four shows that when voters are rational, the closeness of the race doesn't matter—people are no more likely to vote in a close race than in a race where one candidate is ahead by a lopsided margin, even though they have a strong preference about the outcome. The reason is that they believe that one vote is unlikely to change the outcome of an election. Moreover, voting is costly—a would-be voter needs to learn about the candidates and to expend time and effort to get to the polls. Under these conditions, a rational actor can easily decide that abstention is the better choice. In fact, the more interesting question is why a rational actor would ever bother to vote, given the significant costs and miniscule benefits associated with this action.

As this example illustrates, analyzing American politics in terms of individuals and rational choices has two advantages. First, it offers a way to explain political behavior—why, for example, citizens abstain from voting even though they care about who wins. Second, rational-choice assumptions offer a way to predict both individual behavior and aggregate outcomes. Chapter Four, for example, shows that individuals with a strong sense of civic duty and obligation are more likely to vote compared to individuals who lack these beliefs.

This book is not a general introduction to American politics. Rather, it describes a way of thinking about American politics, viewing behavior and outcomes through the lens of rational choice. Moreover, the book shows how this approach provides unique insights into both the shape of American political institutions and how people operate within them. The emphasis is on explaining anomalies—situations where the behavior of voters or politicians contradicts widely held assumptions about what they should be doing, or where the rules and institutions that structure American politics have seemingly unexpected effects.

Preliminary Fundamentals

This book describes American politics in terms of people making rational choices within a set of rules and institutions. This introduction is designed to given you a sense of what this perspective means. Why think about politics in terms of individuals? What is a rational choice? What are institutions?

Individual Rationality

This book describes American politics in terms of rational choices by individuals. Rather than talking in terms of aggregate bodies—"Congress does this" or "Agency X does that"—outcomes will be explained in terms of the actions taken by individuals and the factors that led these individuals to behave as they did.

Why focus on individuals? Because they do the choosing. To say, for example, that the Senate, the Supreme Court, or any other government institution did something is an incorrect statement—none of these groups can do anything without their individual members making choices. The "Senate" is not a person. It is a group of individuals. If we want to understand why a veto was sustained, we need to consider the goals and strategies of each of the hundred senators, along with the rules that determine how the Senate operates.

The same is true for individuals in the electorate. After the 1994 elections, many pundits attributed the Democratic Party's loss of majority status in the House and Senate to the electorate's dissatisfaction with the performance of elected officials from the party. However, there is no beast called the "electorate" that can be interviewed or observed. To paraphrase Christopher Achen, the electorate does not wake up on election day, rub his or her tired eyes, and say, "Today I'm going to vote 52 percent Republican, 47 percent Democrat, and 1 percent Other."[1] Rather, the only way to understand election outcomes is to begin with individual voters, their goals, and their information.

Focusing on individuals carries with it the assumption that participation matters. This book does not consider theories that explain election or policy outcomes in terms of the actions of a small, all-powerful elite. Nor does it discuss theories that say average citizens are powerless to influence what government does. Rather, it assumes that outcomes reflect the wishes and choices of the people who care enough to get involved.

One of the most important assumptions in this book is that people are rational actors and that the choices they make are rational. The term *rationality* carries with it a lot of baggage, such as the idea that rational choices are arrived at unemotionally, along the lines of Mr.

[1]Christopher Achen, "Toward Theories of Data: The State of Political Methodology," in *Political Science: The State of the Discipline*, Ada W. Finifter, ed. (Washington D.C.: American Political Science Association, 1984), p. 82.

Spock and his Vulcan colleagues on *Star Trek*, or that a rational actor never makes mistakes. As used here, *rationality* means something much narrower about the process by which an individual makes decisions.

To say that an individual is *rational* means that she has preferences about the consequences of her behavior and acts on the basis of these preferences. Given a number of possible outcomes, a rational actor can rank the outcomes, from most-liked to least-liked. Faced with a choice among two or more actions, the rational actor takes whatever action is expected to lead to the best-possible outcome or set of outcomes.

Suppose, for example, someone offers you a choice between an apple and an orange. If you're a rational actor (and you should be), you'll respond by thinking about how much you would like each fruit, taking into account taste, vitamin content, and other factors, and then choose the one you like best. Apple lovers choose an apple; orange advocates choose an orange. That's a rational choice—behavior consistent with preferences. (It would also be a rational choice to decline the fruit if you weren't hungry.)

It may make you uncomfortable to think that people are rational. Before you reject the concept, give me another chance to explain it. By labeling people as rational, all I am saying is that they have some idea of what they want and that these ideas drive their behavior. I'm not going to try to explain where preferences come from. Rather, the focus here is on how individuals act on their preferences, on how they try to get what they want from government.

So, you might ask, if a rational action is one that's consistent with my preferences, what's an irrational action? Most people would say that an irrational action is something that's obviously counter productive or harmful—burning a hundred-dollar bill or bungee jumping. In this book, an irrational action is something that's contrary to your preferences, such as choosing an apple when (after taking everything into consideration) you'd prefer an orange. As long as you're choices reflect your preferences, you're a rational actor.

This definition of irrationality implies something profound about what it means to be rational. Simply put, to say that a person behaves rationally does not imply that other people regard the behavior as smart or sensible. All it means is that the person's preferences drive his behavior. In other words, strange as it may seem, it can be rational to bungee jump—as long as you enjoy bungee jumping.

To put it another way, to say that someone is rational says nothing about the content of their preferences. Rational actors can have very strange motivations. For example, in every election, a surprisingly large number of candidates run for office despite having little or no chance of winning. Consider Alan Keyes, who ran in the Republican presidential primaries in the 1996 and 2000 elections. Keyes's strident conservative platform never attracted more than a few percentage points of support, and he never was a serious contender for the nomination.

Does the fact that Keyes had virtually no chance of winning make his decision to run irrational? No. What it suggests is that Keyes did not run to win. Rather, his candidacy was probably designed to gain publicity for the policies that he supports—ending abortion, abolishing the income tax, banning gay marriage, and similar issues. In light of this motivation, Keyes's decision to run was thoroughly rational, as he gained significant media coverage during the campaign. As the headline on his Internet homepage reads, "It's the Principle That Counts."[2]

Rationality also does not imply anything about a person's goodness or morality. For example, Saddam Hussein and the Dalai Lama are both rational actors. Certainly they hold radically different goals and have very different preferences. But their actions can still be explained in terms of preferences, which is all that rationality implies.

To say that people are rational also does not imply that they never make mistakes. As discussed in the next section, voters and elected officials are often uncertain about the consequences of their behavior. Under these conditions, a rational actor might find that her choice did not lead to the best-possible result. This discovery does not mean that the choice was irrational; all it means is that the person lacked some important piece of information at the time of her choice.

Recall the choice between an apple and an orange. You choose the apple because you like eating apples more than you like eating oranges. But after you receive the apple, you find that it has worms in it, and you hate eating worms. If you had known about the apple's condition, you would certainly have chosen the orange. But that conclusion doesn't mean your initial decision was irrational. All it means is that you chose under conditions of uncertainty.

Finally, saying that people make rational choices does not imply that they always invest enough time and resources to insure that they make the right choice. For example, most voters in congressional

[2]www.keyes2000.org

elections know very little about the candidates running for office. Often they decide against learning more about the candidates, even when additional information would help them to decide which candidate would do a better job in office. *Remaining ignorant can be rational.* If a voter doesn't care who wins the election (or cares, but only a little), searching for additional information has significant costs and minimal benefits. Under these conditions, a voter would prefer to remain ignorant, even if this strategy increased the chance that he might vote for an inferior candidate.

Rationality and Political Participation. The assumption of rationality provides a good initial clue as to why people get involved in politics. If people are rational, there must be a reason for their participation, some benefit that they receive; otherwise, they would abstain.

Some political action is no doubt the result of motives that are far outside politics. People work for a political party in order to secure a government job; they vote to impress their partners; or they work for the government because it provides good health insurance.

Leaving these possibilities aside, the expectation in this book is that participation is driven by policy interests. People don't get involved in politics because they are indifferent about public policy. Rather, people participate because they care, sometimes passionately, about making government do the right thing, as they see it. In other words, politics is about people trying to impress their view of how things should be on everyone else.[3]

This book defines political participation extremely broadly. People get involved when they run for office, or serve as an elected official—a legislator, a city councilman, a mayor—or act as a judge or bureaucrat. Ordinary citizens participate when they vote, write letters, or make contributions to elected officials; get involved in a public rally or protest; or work for an interest group or political party. The assumption of rationality implies that all of these behaviors can be traced back to some motive or goal.

In concrete terms, this assumption implies that politics is about issues, such as Will handgun ownership be banned? Will gun safety courses be required? Will laws restricting gun ownership be elimi-

---

[3]For a wider discussion of this point, see William H. Riker, *Liberalism against Populism: A Confrontation between the Theory of Democracy and the Theory of Social Choice* (Prospect Heights, Ohio: Waveland Press, 1982).

nated entirely? The point is not that everyone cares about gun control or that being rational means that you should be concerned; rather, it is that these are the sort of questions that drive political participation and that then become the subject of political debate.

Are People Rational? One of the biggest difficulties with saying that people are rational is the complexity of the real world. How can people be rational, say critics, when the choices they face are so complex—or when they appear to know very little about the consequences of their decisions?

Consider a typical piece of important legislation, such as the Welfare Reform Act of 1996. At the same time the proposal was voted on, many members of Congress had little idea of what the proposal would do if enacted. For example, would the changes mandated by the proposal reduce the number of people on welfare, and if so, by how much? Would welfare recipients find jobs that paid a living wage once their benefits were taken away?

Members of the House and Senate had some idea of the answers to these questions, but no one knew for sure what the impact of the proposal would be. Constituents, who do not have access to the information available to members of Congress and who were probably less interested in the first place, knew even less.

Do these uncertainties mean that legislators and constituents cannot make rational choices about welfare reform—or behave rationally in general? The answer is no. A lack of information doesn't prevent you from behaving rationally. Rather, uncertainty influences both the decisions people make and how they make them.

In the case of welfare reform, uncertainty might lead people to rely on the opinions and endorsements of others rather than gathering additional information on their own. Legislators might, for example, consider what interest groups have to say about the proposal or listen carefully to the opinions of colleagues who know a lot about welfare policy. Constituents, in turn, might allow their representative to make up her own mind about welfare reform, rather than formulating an opinion and demanding that their representative vote in line with it.

Uncertainty might also change the criteria that an individual uses to make a decision. Take voting. Suppose we interview a voter during the 2004 presidential campaign and find that this individual knows very little about the two major-party candidates, Michael Jordan and Courtney Cox, and isn't interested in spending any time gathering additional information.[4] Does the voter's decision to remain uncertain mean that he is not being rational? As noted previously, the answer is no. Rather, the decision implies that the cost of searching for additional information outweighs any benefits this information would provide—a better chance of making the right choice between the candidates.

Does the voter's lack of information mean that he cannot decide which candidate is best? No. But the voter's uncertainty means that he cannot vote on the basis of factors such as the candidates' policy platforms. Rather, the voter may turn to other pieces of information that he gathers in the course of everyday life. That is, the voter's preferences may hinge on his knowledge of Jordan's basketball career or whether he is a devoted fan of the TV show Friends. Such a choice would be perfectly rational, even though it is based on factors that are far outside politics.

Finally, uncertainty often is *asymmetric*—some people know things that others do not. This asymmetry in information creates situations where some people try to resolve their uncertainties, while others try to keep their information a secret. A good example is how Alan Greenspan, chairman of the Federal Reserve Board (the Fed), testifies to Congress regarding interest rates and economic policy. Greenspan's task is to keep the Fed's intentions a secret, because if people on Wall Street knew what the Fed planned to do, they could capitalize on this information in ways that would make it impossible for the Fed to achieve its goals. As a result, his comments are often hard to interpret.

Consider what Chairman Greenspan said about dismal economic conditions in Asian countries during testimony to Congress in late 1997:

> Perhaps it was inevitable that the impressive and rapid growth experienced by the economies in the Asian region would run into a temporary slowdown or pause. But there is no reason that above-average growth in countries that are still in a position to gain from catching up with the prevailing technology cannot persist for a very long time. Nevertheless, rapidly developing, free-market economies periodically can be expected to run into difficulties because investment mistakes are inevitable in any dynamic economy.[5]

---

[4]You can decide which candidate runs as a Democrat and which runs as a Republican.

[5]Testimony of Chairman Alan Greenspan, Committee on Banking and Financial Services, U.S. House of Representatives, November 13, 1997.

What did Greenspan say? In order: (a) Asian countries may be experiencing low rates of economic growth, (b) then again, they may do better than we think, and (c) but even if they're doing well, things can get worse at any time. What did Greenspan say? It's hard to tell.

Greenspan isn't trying to be funny. Nor is he unable to express a clear thought. Rather, his strategy of obfuscation is a thoroughly rational choice given his desire to keep the Fed's intentions a secret.

Obviously, I believe that rational-choice assumptions are a good fit to how people make political choices—I did, after all, choose to write this book around that assumption. But I don't think that you should consider rationality to be a universal truth about human behavior. You should regard this assumption as a mechanism for explaining and predicting the choices people make. Its value lies in the insights it provides—a proposition that will, I hope, be demonstrated in the rest of this book.

Rules and Institutions

While this book explains American politics in terms of individuals and rational choices, it gives an equal emphasis to rules and institutions—the "rules of the game." For the purposes of this book, a *rule* or *institution* is something that affects the number and kinds of choices available to an individual, the consequences of one or more choices, or what an individual knows about these choices or consequences.

What do real-world institutions look like? The analysis of electoral behavior in Chapters Four and Five describes many institutions, ranging from the system of primaries and caucuses used to select Republican and Democratic presidential nominees, to rules that establish how long polling places are open on election day.

Most people think of these institutions as unchanging features of the political process landscape. Most may also think that these institutions are designed to be fair, to give all participants an equal chance of getting what they want. Others may be aware that institutions can help some candidates and hurt others, but feel that these complexities are impossible to understand. By the end of this book, you will see that all three of these intuitions are dead wrong.

The expectation throughout the book is that institutions matter. Keeping voting stations open into the evening, for example, increases turnout—people who were busy during the day can vote on their way home from work. In other words, the rule gives people a new choice. They can vote after work, rather than being constrained to do so at lunchtime.

Institutions can change outcomes as well as choices. For example, changing the polling hours affects who can vote and thus can change the outcome of the election. Suppose, for example, that late voters are predominantly Democrats. If so, extending polling hours will give this party's candidates an advantage.

This simple example about polling hours illustrates two crucial points that will be emphasized throughout the text. For one thing, it shows that seemingly innocuous rules can have an important impact on outcomes that matter, such as who wins an election. People who determine how these institutions operate have an important and little-known power over outcomes. To paraphrase a favorite saying of Representative John Dingell, a senior member of the U.S. House, "If you let me write procedure and I let you write substance, I'll beat you every time."[6] In other words, the ability to determine how votes are cast or counted often matters more than the ability to determine what's being voted on.

The example also shows that choices involving rules are really choices about outcomes. Late polling hours favor Democratic candidates; closing the polls early favors Republicans. For the average politician, deciding whether to support an extension of polling hours doesn't involve normative issues, such as whether keeping the hours short encourages voting, or whether people should be allowed to vote at their convenience. Rather, the question is, "Do I want to help elect Republicans or Democrats?"

The message of this book is that both in politics and in life, you should not evaluate institutions in the abstract. Rather, you should ask, "What kind of outcome is each rule likely to produce and which set do I prefer?" The battle over political institutions, both large and small, is really a battle over public policy.

Later chapters demonstrate how politicians have an outcome-centered view of institutions and rules. Their public pronouncements about proposed institutional changes may stress normative arguments—for example, that polling stations should be open late to allow people to exercise their civic responsibility without having to take time off from work. However, when making institutional choices, most politicians ask a more basic question: Which institution will

[6]Quoted in Phil Duncan, *Politics in America* (Washington, D.C.: Congressional Quarterly Press, 1983), p. 800.

help them achieve their goals? Will keeping the polls open late help them win the election or aid in the election of candidates who think the way they do? The analysis here follows this lead. The goal is to understand how existing rules and institutions shape the choices facing voters, politicians, and other political actors, as well as to explain changes in these institutions in terms of rational choices.

The Plan of the Book

The structure of this book echoes these two themes: individual rationality and institutions. Each chapter focuses on a small number of examples or behaviors, with the goal of explaining these phenomena in detail rather than making a comprehensive survey of American politics.

Chapter Two shows how the rules matter. The focus is on the 1912 presidential election and various methods that could have been used to select the winning candidate. While each method has certain advantages and disadvantages, all of them are defensible choices. The critical insight is that each method yields a different outcome—a different winner of the election. This example illustrates how politicians can stack the deck, choosing institutions and rules that favor the outcomes they prefer.

Chapter Three examines the problems that rational individuals face when trying to cooperate to their mutual benefit, either in the formation of a political party or interest group, or when making legislative deals in Congress. Cooperation under these conditions requires a solution to two similar problems. First, why should rational, self-interested individuals help a group, when they benefit from the group's success regardless of what they do? Second, why should the same rational, self-interested individuals carry out the terms of a legislative bargain, when they can do better by reneging?

The analysis in this chapter shows that some groups, by virtue of who they are, what they are trying to do, or their ability to construct institutional solutions, will find it easier to achieve and sustain both kinds of cooperation. For others, cooperation is doomed from the start.

Chapter Four deals with voters' decisions in elections. The biggest surprise is that abstention is a rational choice. In fact, if the only benefit from voting were the ability to influence who gets elected, very few people would bother. What is the rational explanation for voting?

The answer is that citizens receive other kinds of benefits from voting, such as social approval or self-esteem from fulfilling their civic duty.

The second part of Chapter Four focuses on how voters gather information about candidates. Here, the question is Why do voters often use a candidate's physical appearance or record outside politics to assess her abilities? The chapter shows that voters' information-gathering strategies are sensitive to both search costs (the cost of gathering information) and credibility (whether seemingly valid information can be taken seriously). These considerations explain the strategies followed by many real-world voters, confirming that their behavior is eminently rational.

Chapter Five looks at how candidates campaign. The first half explains how candidates choose their campaign platform—what they promise to do if elected. Here the puzzle is why candidates often end up sounding alike, offering very similar promises to the electorate. This behavior is no surprise once it is recognized that most candidates want to win their election. This goal motivates each candidate to advocate positions that are favored by moderate voters in her constituency, even if this choice leaves her sounding like her opponent.

The second part of Chapter Five focuses on elections as an institution that enables voters to reward representatives who have done good things in office and punish those who have not. However, many real-world voters refuse to use this mechanism, allowing their legislators to make choices for them. Why is trust a rational choice for these constituents? The chapter describes the conditions under which trust benefits constituents and shows that these conditions match the circumstances under which trust is observed in the social world.

Congressional institutions and behavior are the focus in Chapter Six. The first half of the chapter considers why members of Congress enact wasteful, inefficient "pork barrel" legislation, proposals that spend large amounts of funds for projects of dubious worth. The chapter also examines why constituents reward pork barreling. The answer lies in the standards that constituents use to evaluate their representative's behavior. Pork barrel projects are not enacted because legislators favor them on their merits; rather, they exist because delivering these benefits makes constituents happy and thereby helps members get reelected.

The second part of Chapter Six analyzes a fundamental congressional institution, the committee system. Committees help members of Congress to make well-informed decisions. They also allow members to trade away influence over policies that don't matter to them in return for control over policies they care about. The chapter shows how members use rules and the assignment process to achieve both of these goals.

Chapter Seven explores two examples of how institutions shape rational choices involving the executive branch of government. The first example focuses on bargaining between the president and members of Congress, and on the usefulness of the president's veto power. The chapter shows how the power conferred by the veto varies with factors such as whether the president likes the status quo (the outcome that results if no law is enacted) and the distribution of policy preferences in Congress. Sometimes the veto matters—the fact that the president has this power changes the outcome of legislative action. Other times, the president's veto gives him no power over the legislative process.

The second part of Chapter Seven deals with congressional oversight and with the charge that members of Congress ignore their responsibility to monitor what bureaucrats are doing. Are bureaucrats free agents, able to act as they think best, even when their decisions run contrary to congressional intent? The answer is no. The absence of full-blown investigations reflects a choice about how to perform oversight, not neglect of this activity. Members rely on people and organizations outside Congress to keep them informed about bureaucratic misdeeds and have modified various institutions to facilitate oversight from the outside. This strategy lowers the cost of oversight, as well as making oversight more beneficial to legislators in both policy and political terms.

Chapter Eight focuses on the Supreme Court. Members of the Court are usually thought of as being above politics and strategizing. This intuition is incorrect. The first part of Chapter Eight shows how a chief justice, Warren Burger, regularly switched votes in order to maximize his influence over judicial decisions. The second section shows how the Court's power of judicial review provides an additional institutional mechanism for controlling unelected bureaucrats.

The concluding chapter, Chapter Nine summarizes all of these findings, highlighting the value of studying politics through a rational-choice lens and thinking about political institutions and rules in terms of their effect on choices and outcomes.

2

Deciding How to Decide

This chapter examines rules of procedure and other political institutions. The goal is to illustrate a central theme of this book. You will find here that institutions do more than specify how the political process works—for instance, when elections are held and how ballots are counted. Rather, rules and institutions have an independent effect on outcomes. How you decide often affects what you decide.

The focus here is on voting rules, the methods used by groups of people to make some joint decision. Typically, people involved in decision making tend to overlook the procedures that govern how the decision will be made. It is as though they think, "Who cares how we decide? The outcome will be determined by what we want, rather than how our votes are counted."

This intuition would find no support among politicians. Their view of the world is summed up by the quote from John Dingell cited above: "If you let me write procedure [i.e., determine how alternatives are voted on] and I let you write substance [i.e., define the set of alternatives], I'll beat you every time." This chapter explains what Dingell is talking about. For any group decision, such as an election or a legislative proceeding, there are many seemingly fair methods by which to count votes, each with its own advantages and disadvantages. However, these rules often will not produce the same winner—the same group choice. In other words, by selecting the method of decision, you can change the outcome.

This theme is developed through this chapter using a running example, the 1912 presidential election. Using the electoral rules of that time (similar to those used today), the election was won by the Democratic candidate, Woodrow Wilson. If, however, the United States in 1912 selected presidents using a system of approval voting, the Republican candidate, William Howard Taft, would have been elected. And if presidents were elected in 1912 using the Borda method (see pages 22–24), the independent candidate, Theodore Roosevelt, would have won.

As you will see, the Borda method and approval voting are not obscure or flawed methods—they are used here because they provide exceptionally clear illustrations of the ability of institutions to perturb group decision making. The impact of rules and procedures on outcomes is inherent in group decision making. Even if you only look at ostensibly fair voting rules, different methods yield different outcomes.

If different rules produce different outcomes, can one be identified as better than all the rest based on some definition of fairness? The answer is no. No voting system can satisfy a set of intuitively reasonable, fairly modest requirements. Many commonly used voting rules violate at least one of these requirements. For example, as we shall see in this chapter, no voting system ensures that a majority of voters will endorse the outcome of an election.

These findings have important implications for understanding the rules and institutions that determine how politics works. If different rules can generate different outcomes, then rational actors will be concerned both with casting votes and with determining how their votes are counted. If so, fights over the selection of rules are not abstract debates over principles. Rather, they are fights over outcomes, fights to select rules that favor one kind of outcome and work to the disadvantage of others.

The Strategy of Choice:
The Case of the 1912 Presidential Elections

When analyzing decision making in politics or elsewhere, the first step is to define who is doing the choosing and what options they are choosing among. This analysis begins with the preferences held by voters in the 1912 presidential election, as described in Table 2.1.

TABLE 2.1
Voters Preferences in the 1912 Presidential Elections.

Group	Size	Preferences
Wilsonians	42% (6.3 million)	Wilson, Roosevelt, Taft, Debs
Rooseveltians	28% (4.1 million)	Roosevelt, Taft, Wilson, Debs
Taftites	23% (3.5 million)	Taft, Wilson, Roosevelt, Debs
Debsians	7% (900 thousand)	Debs, Roosevelt, Taft, Wilson

There were four candidates in the election:

• Woodrow Wilson, the Democratic Party nominee
• William Howard Taft, then president and the Republican Party nominee
• Theodore Roosevelt, ex-president and former Republican, running as the nominee of the Bull Moose Party
• Eugene Debs, nominee of the Socialist Party

The table gives the preference orderings for the supporters of each candidate. For example, Wilsonians are voters who rate Woodrow Wilson as the best candidate in the election. They make up 42 percent of the electorate.[1] Their preference ordering has Wilson in first place and Roosevelt as the second-place alternative. This ordering implies that these voters prefer Wilson to any of the other three candidates, but prefer Roosevelt to Taft and Roosevelt to Debs. They also prefer Taft, the third candidate in their preference ordering, to Debs, who they rank fourth and last.

The other groups have different preferences across the four candi-

---

[1] As you will see, the percentage of voters that hold each of these preference orderings can be deduced from the votes cast in the 1912 election.

dates. Rooseveltians, who make up 27 percent of the electorate, like Teddy Roosevelt the best, with a preference ordering of Roosevelt first, Taft second, Wilson third, and Debs fourth. Taftites (24 percent) want to reelect the incumbent, and prefer Taft first, Wilson second, Roosevelt third, and Debs fourth. Finally, Debsians (7 percent) prefer Debs first, Roosevelt second, Taft third, and Wilson last.

As discussed in Chapter One, these voters are assumed to behave as rational actors. In this context, rationality means that a voter prefers to elect a candidate who is positioned high in his preference ordering compared to one who is lower.[2] Wilsonians, for example, would rather see Wilson elected than any other candidate. They also prefer the election of Roosevelt to Taft or Debs, and Taft to Debs. How a voter acts on his preferences depends on the voting method used in the election.

How Special Is This Example?

Since the point of this chapter is to show how the rules matter, you may be suspicious that I have cooked up this example to make sure my results match my claims.[3]

At one level, the answer is I haven't. The preferences in Table 2.1 are consistent with the actual results of the 1912 election—Wilson received 42 percent of votes cast, Roosevelt 27 percent, and so on. The preference orderings fit what scholars know about opinions held at the time by different groups in the population.

I have reduced the number of preference orderings in the example by dividing voters into only four groups. That's a simplification of reality. It's almost certainly true, for example, that not all Wilsonians wanted Roosevelt to win if Wilson did not. Some of these voters may have had Taft in second place, or even Debs. Similarly, some Taftites

[2]Remember that women could not vote in the 1912 election. The franchise was not extended to women in the United States until 1920!

[3]This example is also simplified in that it considers a fixed set of voters and a fixed set of alternatives. In the real world, these factors are often up for grabs. For example, an individual cannot run for President or Vice President unless she is a U.S. citizen, 35 years old or older, and born in the United States. While these rules are part of the Constitution, they are not set in stone and could be changed at any time. With regard to altering the set of voters, this tactic is sometimes used in towns that have a high percentage of college students. Local politicians often lobby the Board of Elections to discourage or prohibit students from registering to vote, as a means of preventing students from banding together and electing a block of like-minded candidates to the town council, school board, and other offices.

may have preferred Roosevelt to Wilson, rather than the opposite assumed in Table 2.1. However, these simplification of preferences would generate much the same results as those you see here.

The place where your suspicions might be justified is in the selection of this particular example. Why examine the 1912 presidential election? The answer is simple: This example highlights the impact that rules can have on outcomes.[4] This impact does not occur in all elections, presidential or otherwise. Even so, the fact that the selection of rules sometimes has a strong influence on group decisions makes this factor an important thing to study, even if these effects do not always occur.

Different Ways to Elect Presidents

This section describes the current rules for electing presidents in the United States, as well as two alternative voting systems: approval voting and the Borda method. The goal is to show two things: First, each of these methods is a viable, sensible way to choose a president. If anything, the current rules are the most complicated and cumbersome of the three.

Second and more importantly, each method would have produced a different winner if it had been used to decide the 1912 presidential election.

The Current Rules: Plurality Voting and the Electoral College. If you ask an average voter how presidents are elected in contemporary America, she is likely to say that the election works as follows: each voter votes for exactly one candidate, then the votes are counted across the entire nation, and the candidate who receives the most votes wins.

This picture is wrong. To begin with, citizens don't vote for presidential candidates. Rather, they choose between slates of electors

[4]The 1912 election is also worth studying because it shows us what presidential elections are like when there are more than two viable candidates. Traditionally, third-party candidates have little chance of winning in American presidential elections, but this regularity may be at an end. A third-party candidate for president, Ross Perot, received 19 percent of votes cast in 1992 and about 10 percent in 1996. His party may do even better in 2000: as of late 1999, possible nominees included Jesse "The Body" Ventura (ex-pro wrestler and governor of Minnesota), real estate developer and well-known publicity hound Donald Trump, and the actor Warren Beatty. What are the pros and cons of different voting rules when there are three viable candidates? Analyzing the 1912 election is a good way to address this question.

who are pledged to support a particular candidate. (Ballots highlight the presidential candidate's name, but usually state in small print that voters are really choosing electors.) The number of electors for a state equals the number of House members from the state plus the number of Senators.

When the election is held, votes are counted by state. In each state, the slate of electors that receives the most votes (a *plurality*) is declared the winner. The members of winning elector slates assemble in early December in Washington, D.C., to select the next president. They meet as the *electoral college*, and there vote for their preferred presidential candidate. The candidate who wins a majority of votes from the electoral college becomes the new president. If no candidate receives a majority from the college, the members of the House of Representatives choose the winner using a set of obscure procedures.

This description of presidential elections doesn't fit the average voter's conception of how presidents are chosen. Upon hearing the details of the how Americans elect their president, responses generally fall into three categories:

- "Aren't presidential elections held on the first Tuesday in November?" Not really. That election chooses members of the electoral college, who make the actual decision about a month later.
- "What if electors ignore their pledges and choose whoever they want?" The answer is, nobody knows. Renegade votes are cast from time to time, although there have never been enough to change the result of the election.
- "Can a candidate win a majority of electoral votes without winning a majority of votes actually cast by citizens?" This result is possible, although it hasn't happened in over one hundred years.

Clearly, the current system for electing presidents is complicated and leaves several important questions unanswered.

The advantage of the current system lies in the simplicity of the choice voters make. Each voter votes once and only once. All they have to decide is which candidate they like the best—which one is at the top of their preference ordering. From the perspective of a voter, presidential elections look the same as elections to most other federal, state, and local offices.

The simplicity of the current system is also a drawback. By only allowing voters to reveal who they like the most, instead of their full preference ordering, this system can generate outcomes that many voters consider inferior.

Consider a Rooseveltian in the 1912 election. By voting for Roosevelt, this voter can indicate that this candidate is at the top of his preference ordering. However, there's no way for this voter to indicate that he ranks Taft second, ahead of Wilson and Debs. This inability is particularly problematic for the voter, because the winner of the election, Wilson, is third best from the voter's perspective. This voter would like to cast a vote that expresses strong support for Roosevelt, qualified support for Taft, opposition to Wilson, and strong opposition to Debs. Under the plurality system, there is no way to express this preference.

How did plurality voting and the electoral college work in the 1912 presidential election? Table 2.2 shows the number and percentage of the popular vote (voters cast by citizens) received by each candidate, as well as the number and percentage of electoral votes.

Table 2.2
The 1912 Presidential Elections Using Plurality Voting and the Electoral College

Candidate	Popular Vote		Electoral Vote	
	Number	Percent	Number	Percent
Wilson	6,293,152	42	435	82
Roosevelt	4,127,788	28	88	17
Taft	3,486,333	23	8	2
Debs	901,255	7	0	0

As the table shows, Woodrow Wilson received the most popular votes (over six million, or about 42 percent), as well as a majority of votes in the electoral college (435, or about 82 percent), and was therefore elected president.

The Borda Method. The *Borda*[5] *method* was designed to allow a voter's choice to reflect her entire preference ordering of all the candidates. Using this method, each individual submits a ballot that awards points to the various alternatives under consideration, with

[5]The Borda method was invented by Jean Charles Borda, a nineteenth-century French mathematician.

higher-ranked candidates getting more points and lower-ranked candidates getting fewer. If there are four alternatives, such as in 1912
elections, the top-ranked alternative in a voter's ordering gets three
points, the second-ranked alternative gets two points, the third-
ranked, one point, and the fourth and lowest-ranked alternative, no
points.[6]

As this example indicates, the Borda method takes an individual's
single vote and divides it across all of the possible alternatives. Candidates who are ranked higher by the voter receive a larger share of her
vote, and lower-ranked candidates receive a smaller share. Each individual's ballot reflects her evaluation of all of the alternatives under
consideration.

Once all the Borda ballots are submitted, the points given to each
alternative are added up. The candidate who receives the most points
is the winner.

To see how the Borda count works, consider a Debsian, who
prefers Debs first, Roosevelt second, Taft third, and Wilson fourth.
This voter's ballot would allocate three points to Debs, two to Roosevelt, one to Taft, and none to Wilson. In contrast, Wilsonians, who
put Wilson first, Roosevelt second, Taft third, and Debs last, would
allocate three points to Wilson, two to Roosevelt, one to Taft, and
none to Debs.

The Borda method is not used in American national elections.
However, some departments in American universities use the Borda
method to make hiring decisions. And many law and business schools
use this procedure to make both admission and financial-aid decisions.

Perhaps the best-known use of the Borda method is in the weekly
coaches' polls conducted by *USA Today*, Associated Press, and various other media outlets. These polls are used to rank intercollegiate
athletic teams. Each participating coach submits a weekly list of the
teams that they think are among the twenty-five best in their sport,
ranked from number one to number twenty-five. These ballots are
then translated into points awarded to different teams (a team gets
twenty-four points every time it's first on someone's ballot, twenty-
three points every time it's second, and so on), which are then added

---

[6]Here's the general rule for the Borda method. If there are n outcomes being voted
on, each voter allocates n-1 points to the highest outcome in her preference ordering, n-2 to the second-highest, and so on through the ordering to the voter's least-
preferred outcome, which is not awarded any points.

up and transformed into the weekly ranking that appears in your newspaper.

What would have happened if the 1912 elections had been held using the rules that rank college football teams? The results are shown in Table 2.3.

TABLE 2.3
Outcome of the 1912 Elections Using the Borda Method

Candidate	Number of Points
Roosevelt	30,000,000
Wilson	29,700,000
Taft	25,800,000
Debs	2,700,000

Table 2.3 reports Borda-method point totals for each of the candidates: Wilson, Roosevelt, Taft, and Debs. (The calculations needed to arrive at these totals, which are based on the data in Table 2.1, are omitted.)

The table shows that if the Borda method had been used in the 1912 presidential election, then Roosevelt would have been the winner. He received just over 30 million points to Wilson's 29 million and change. Note that Wilson received 42 percent and Roosevelt 28 percent of votes cast using plurality voting and the electoral college, which also gave Wilson an overwhelming majority of electoral votes—82 percent. Even so, Wilson's support does not translate into a victory if the Borda method is used to select a winner.

The finding that Roosevelt would have won under the Borda method while Wilson was the victor using the electoral college system is the first suggestion that the rules matter. Someone with the power to decide how votes were counted in 1912 could have changed the outcome of the election. For example, a Rooseveltian could have ensured the election of his favored candidate by mandating the Borda method, while a Wilsonian would have secured Wilson's election by sticking with plurality voting and the electoral college.

Approval Voting. While the Borda method allows an individual to cast votes that take account of his entire preference ordering, this advantage comes with added complexity. Individuals using the Borda method must spend a significant amount of time filling out a complex ballot. And before an individual casts a Borda vote, he has to construct a preference ordering of all the candidates, deciding which candidate he likes the most, which one second-best, and so on.

These sorts of complexities suggest that the Borda method might be too cumbersome to be used in American national elections. Even if voters are rational, the costs involved with determining their Borda ballot may cause them to be less than thoughtful about ranking alternatives, particularly those at the bottom of their preference ordering.[7] This section discusses a voting rule that splits the difference between the simplicity of plurality voting and the complexities of the Borda method: approval voting.[8]

Under a system of *approval voting*, each participant can cast a variable number of votes: as few as one and as many as there are candidates. The idea is that people can vote for as many candidates as they consider acceptable, as many as they approve of. The votes are then counted, and the candidate with the most votes wins.

Suppose a Wilsonian likes Wilson best but thinks that Roosevelt and Taft would also make good presidents. Under approval voting, the individual would cast three votes, one each for Wilson, Roosevelt, and Taft, and none for Debs. With simple plurality voting, this individual could only indicate his support for Wilson, and could not express his approval of Roosevelt or Taft.

Of course, voters using approval voting do not have to vote for multiple candidates. A rational voter may decide to "bullet vote"— vote for only one candidate. For example, a Debsian who thinks Debs is great and all the other candidates are terrible can cast a single vote for Debs and withhold support from everyone else.

As these examples suggest, approval voting allows an individual's vote to reflect, in a simple and easy-to-understand way, her feelings about all of the candidates in the election. Moreover, approval voting doesn't require a lot of thought—it reduces the cost of figuring out how to vote. A voter doesn't have to consider how much she likes each candidate. All the voter has to do is figure out which of the candidates is above some threshold or line. In essence, she has to answer the question, "Which candidates do I think would make a good president," and vote for however many pass this test.

---

[7] Chapter Four contains a detailed discussion of the cost of voting and its impact on the behavior of rational voters.

[8] See Steven J. Brams and Peter C. Fishburn, 1983 *Approval Voting* (Boston: Bilkhauser, 1983).

What would have happened if approval voting had been used in the 1912 election? The answer depends on how many candidates were considered acceptable by different groups of voters. While approval voting has never been used in a major U.S. election, experiments suggest that in an election involving four or so alternatives, most voters will vote for one or perhaps two alternatives. With this intuition in mind, suppose that the members of the four groups in Table 2.1 cast approval votes as follows:

Wilsonians: Vote for Wilson only
Rooseveltians: Vote for Roosevelt and Taft
Taftites: Vote for Taft only
Debsians: Vote for Debs and Roosevelt

These votes produce the totals shown in Table 2.4.

TABLE 2.4
Outcome of the 1912 Elections Using Approval Voting

Candidate	Number of Votes
Taft	7,614,121
Wilson	6,293,152
Roosevelt	5,029,043
Debs	901,255

Under approval voting, with votes cast as described above, Taft would have won the election with a total of 7,614,121 votes (4,127,788 from Taftites and 3,486,333 from Rooseveltians). Wilson would have come in second with 6,293,152 votes, all from Wilsonians. Roosevelt would have gotten 4,127,788 votes from Rooseveltians and 901,255 from Debsians for a total of 5,029,043, which puts him in third place. And Debs would be last with 901,255 votes.

Three Rules, Three Outcomes

A look across the three voting methods described in this chapter—plurality voting plus the electoral college, the Borda method, and approval voting—highlights the influence that rules have on outcomes. Each method produces a different winner for the 1912 election. Wilson won the election held using plurality voting and the electoral college. But Roosevelt would have won had the Borda method been used, and Taft would have become president given approval voting.

This finding highlights the enormous power held by *agenda setters,* people who can impose a method of decision making on a group. If, for example, someone had good information on voter preferences and could determine the method of voting used in elections, that person would be a dictator. He could ensure the victory of his preferred candidate (or, in the case of Debsians, his second-place preference) by picking the right voting rule. Thus, a Wilsonian would select the current system, which elects Wilson. Similarly, a Rooseveltian would choose the Borda method, while a Taftite would pick approval voting.

You may question whether people would choose to alter the rules that govern group decisions. Why not stick to voting on alternatives using whatever rules are in place, rather than proposing a different way to count votes? The answer is simple. If you believe that people who are rational actors have preferences across the alternatives being voted on, then you should expect them to do everything they can to ensure that their favored alternative wins. In other words, the fact that voters are rational motivates them to cast the right vote—a vote that helps their favored alternative win.[9] But the same motivation should lead them to fight for rules changes that have the same effect.

Of course, one person can't determine how presidents are elected. Changing those rules requires amending the Constitution, which is a long and complicated procedure. Even so, this example illustrates that all voting rules are not created equal. Rules that are part of the Constitution are hard to change, but this fact doesn't make them neutral or fair. It just means that the bias they introduce is a fixed part of the political landscape, at least for the short term.

Moreover, in many real-world situations, it's easy to change the rules. Even in elections, some rules, such as registration requirements for voters or rules governing ballot access for candidates, are often changed from year to year. And in most situations where a group decision is required, voting rules are typically set without much thought and only when needed. Such situations invite manipulation by people who know how the rules matter.

For example, suppose you share an apartment or dorm suite with

[9]Chapter Four discusses an exception to this statement: when voting is costly in terms of time or other resources, an individual might abstain even if she likes some alternatives better than others.

several other people. You want to set a date for a party. How should you decide? Before you set the date, you and your friends first need to determine how to arrive at this decision. In situations like these, people who know how voting rules work, and who can make good guesses about the preferences of their friends, can easily alter the outcome by suggesting a voting method that favors their preferred alternative (we'll come back to this example later in the chapter).

The ability to alter a group's decision by changing the rules can transform the process of choice into a meaningless exercise. Suppose you are in a situation that resembles the 1912 election. If you control how the decision is made, you can arrange things so that your preferred alternative wins (unless you are a Debsian, in which case you can get your second-place alternative). And you can manipulate the outcome without choosing a blatantly unfair method of voting, pressuring people to vote as you want, or ignoring votes cast against your preferred alternative.[10] To the world, you may seem democratic and impartial, but the power to select the method of voting makes you a dictator. The participants can vote however they like, but the result is preordained.

Thus, the fact that people are rational, and can seem to influence a group decision by voting, does not imply that they have any influence over the result, even if they cast votes that are rational in light of their preferences. People have this sort of influence only when, in addition to casting votes, they can determine the method of voting and the alternatives being voted on.

Do these problems always arise? No. Sometimes voters' preferences are such that the same alternative wins regardless of the method of decision. (For instance, suppose that almost all voters in 1912 were Wilsonians.) The point is that counting votes is not as simple as most people think. You cannot be sure that the outcome of an election or other group decision has been biased by the rules used to count votes, but neither can you be sure that this bias does not exist.

What About Sophisticated Behavior?

Thus far, I have assumed that voters behave sincerely, meaning that they always vote based on their true preferences. That is, a Wilsonian

---

[10]In other words, you don't have to use Parent's Antidemocratic Tactic Number 12: "The family will decide by voting, but kids get one vote each, while mom and dad get 100 votes between them."

always votes for Wilson in a plurality contest and, if he considers Wilson and Roosevelt to be acceptable, casts approval votes for both candidates. However, some voting rules create opportunities for *sophisticated voting* behavior, where a voter might do better by misrepresenting his preferences. In other words, a rational voter might do things that look irrational at first glance. A full description of sophisticated behavior is beyond the scope of this book, but this section describes the concept of sophistication as well as its implications.

To understand how sophistication works, consider Wilsonians voting under the approval system. As described earlier, these voters see Wilson as the only acceptable candidate, and cast approval votes only for him. However, when everyone behaved sincerely as described earlier, Taft wins the election—not a happy result for the Wilsonians, as Taft is their third-place alternative.

Can the Wilsonians generate a better result by casting votes that are contrary to their preferences? The answer is yes. Suppose they voted for Roosevelt as well as Wilson. Their additional votes for Roosevelt would change the outcome of the election—Roosevelt would win rather than Taft. Why do the Wilsonians want to elect Roosevelt? Because they like him more than Taft, even though they consider both candidates to be unacceptable. Thus, by misrepresenting their preferences, Wilsonians can produce a better result than if they behave sincerely and only vote for Wilson.

This example shows that once a method of decision has been set, opportunities for strategic behavior still exist. Sincere behavior—voting in accordance with one's preferences—may not be an optimal strategy for a rational voter. A sophisticated strategy, whereby an individual misrepresents her preferences at some point in the decision process, may produce a preferable result.

The possibility of sophisticated behavior also highlights another theme of this book, the importance of information in politics. Most voters consider information about candidates to be sufficient for decision making. For group decisions, though, information also includes knowledge of how a voting method works or data on the preferences held by other voters. A voter who is thinking of behaving sophisticatedly under, say, the Borda method needs to understand the details of how votes are converted into points, as well as information on the preferences of other voters. The voter also needs to have a good idea of how other voters are expected to vote, and whether they will respond to attempts to shape outcomes with sophisticated strategies of their own.

The Impossibility of Fairness in Voting

The fact that different voting rules can yield different outcomes often leads people to consider other criteria for deciding how to count votes. One seemingly sensible idea is to decide in advance on a set of requirements that describe a "good" or "fair" voting rule, then search for a rule that satisfies these criteria.

Unfortunately, analyses of voting rules have found no method that satisfies even a small set of essential fairness criteria. This problem does not arise because people are irrational, unwilling to compromise, or insufficiently imaginative when searching for a new method of decision making. Rather, even when voters are well informed and fully rational, the problem arises because of the preferences that these voters bring to their decision.

That voting rules may not satisfy even simple fairness criteria can be demonstrated by considering one important example, the majority-preferred criteria. This criteria states that a voting rule is fair only if it produces majority-preferred outcomes. That is, the alternative that wins when the method is used is always majority-preferred to each of the losing alternatives.

To see what this criteria means, suppose you and your friends face a choice among three potential party dates: Friday night, Saturday night, or Monday night. (I assume that other nights are out of the question because of your study schedules.)

Suppose that the voting method you use selects Friday night as the time for the party. The Friday option is the majority-preferred alternative if a majority of you and your friends prefer Friday to Saturday, and if a majority prefers Friday to Monday. If (and this is a big if) your voting rule always produced majority-preferred alternatives, regardless of the preferences held by you and your friends, then this rule would satisfy the majority-preferred criteria.

The majority-preferred criteria captures something about elections that most voters would likely regard as essential. Most people think that "majorities rule"—a coalition of voters that's a majority should get what they want from a group decision. That is, they should be able to elect their preferred candidate or, at a minimum, should not get stuck with a candidate they don't like.

The majority-preferred criterion reflects this intuition. Suppose a voting method satisfies this criterion. Then every time the method is used, a majority will be happy with the result. Conversely, suppose a voting rule does not meet the majority-preferred criteria. Then at least some of the time, after a winning alternative is chosen, a majority of voters would rather have one of the losing alternatives. For example, suppose you used a voting rule that generated Saturday night as the date for the party, even though a majority preferred Friday to Saturday. Most people would conclude that something was wrong with a voting rule that produced this result.

Regardless of how sensible the majority-preferred criteria seems, there is, in fact, no voting method that ensures that this requirement is met. The problem is not a defect in how votes are counted, or limits on how rational people are in the real world. Rather, the problem lies with the preferences that people bring (or might bring) to the decision.

Consider Table 2.5, which takes the voter preferences in Table 2.1 and shows how they add up into majority preferences between pairs of candidates.

TABLE 2.5
A Voting Cycle

Majority preference across pair	*Voters who favor each candidate*
Wilson preferred to Roosevelt	Wilson: Wilsonians, Taftites
	Roosevelt: Rooseveltians, Debsians
Roosevelt preferred to Taft	Roosevelt: Wilsonians, Rooseveltians, Debsians
	Taft: Taftites
Taft preferred to Wilson	Taft: Rooseveltians, Taftites, Debsians
	Wilson: Wilsonians

For example, a majority of voters in 1912 (Wilsonians and Taftites) prefer Wilson to Roosevelt. Similarly, a majority (Wilsonians, Rooseveltians, and Debsians) prefers Roosevelt to Taft, and a majority (Rooseveltians, Taftites, and Debsians) prefers Taft to Wilson. The table omits the fourth candidate, Debs, as a majority prefers any of the other three candidates to him.

Taken together, these data reveal a surprising result: Regardless of which of these three candidate wins, a majority prefers one of the losing candidates. If Wilson is selected, a majority prefers Taft. If Roosevelt is chosen, a majority prefers Wilson. And if Taft wins, a majority would rather have Roosevelt.

The situation described in Table 2.5 is a *voting cycle*. Cycles do not always exist—it depends on voters' preferences. However, no method of voting can prevent cycles. The only solution is to forbid voters to consider some alternatives or to tell them they cannot hold certain kinds of preference orderings. Since the former is antidemocratic and the latter is impossible, cycles are a fact of life.

The fact that voting cycles cannot be eradicated implies that satisfaction is not guaranteed in politics. Even when individuals are free to decide which alternatives to consider and how they will vote, their deliberations may not produce majority-preferred results. The problem is not that people behave irrationally, don't propose the right alternatives, or choose bad methods of voting. It is that situations can arise where no voting rule can produce a majority-preferred result from the preferences that people bring to the group decision, even if they are fully rational and have complete freedom to decide how their votes will be counted.

So, you might say, what if I abandon the majority-preferred criteria? Are there other fairness criteria that can be used to identify a good voting rule? Here, again, the search turns up empty. One of the most influential results in the study of voting methods, *Arrow's theorem*, begins by describing some minimal fairness criteria, then shows that no voting system satisfies all of these criteria.[11]

Some of the criteria in Arrow's theorem describe fundamental features of democracy. For example, one criteria states that individuals are free to hold whatever preferences they wish and are completely free to cast whatever vote they want to. A second requirement is nondictatorship: No one individual can always get what he wants, regardless of the preferences held by other voters. Again, this requirement seems fundamental for a democracy.

Arrow's theorem also states that a fair voting scheme must produce

[11]Arrow's theorem was developed by Kenneth Arrow, who later won a Nobel Prize in economics. Depending on who does the counting, there are between five and seven criteria listed in the theorem.

a transitive ordering of all the alternatives that are under consideration. *Transitivity* is similar to the majority-preferred criteria described earlier: It means that the voting method produces a clear winner, and no group of voters large enough to select a different alternative wants to do so. Or, to put it another way, if a voting method always produces a transitive ordering, voting cycles will never arise.

When Arrow began his work, he expected to develop an existence result, that is, he would show that some voting methods satisfied all of his criteria. What he found was an impossibility result: No method of voting satisfies all of Arrow's criteria. In other words, the case of the 1912 presidential election is not an exception. Rather, it highlights a gap in our intuitions about voting and about politics. Democracy itself embodies the potential for manipulation. As a result, politics is not so much a search for the common good, as it is a battle to shape rules in order to determine whose version of the good prevails.

Arrow's theorem also implies that dissatisfaction is a fact of life in politics and does not arise because the rules are biased or because voters are unable to make rational choices. Often, media coverage of American politics highlights the fact that the political process has produced policy outcomes that are contrary to the interests held by a majority of the electorate. In the 1980s, this sort of coverage focused on the rapidly increasing national debt. The late-1990s version highlighted the Social Security and Medicare programs. The common theme in this coverage is that something is wrong—that the rules governing elections are biased against candidates who wanted to help the majority of citizens or that voters are simply unable to vote for candidates who will act in their interests.

Arrow's theorem suggests a different explanation for these apparent failures of the political process. Even when voters are fully informed and completely rational, and even when the rules governing how votes are counted are as fair as they can be, majorities may not be happy with the results of the election. There's no way to eliminate this problem—it's inherent in democracy itself.

Summary

The rules matter. Decisions about how to decide often shape, and can even determine, what is decided. Whether the participants know it or not, debates over how choices will be made are really arguments over which alternative will ultimately be selected. This conclusion has been described here for voting rules, but as later chapters will illustrate, it is equally true everywhere else in politics.

The findings illustrate the importance of information in politics. A participant in a group decision gains extra power if she can determine how votes are counted, or if she knows enough to behave with sophistication once a method has been chosen. Power also accrues to people who are well informed about how different rules and procedures work, and who have good information about the preferences of their opponents.

One common response to these findings is to argue that there exists some undiscovered voting rule that everyone would see as the fairest, best way to make group decisions. However, Arrow's theorem has proven that no voting method, known or unknown, can meet a set of minimal fairness criteria. In other words, while scholars don't know everything about voting, they know that no perfect method exists. The absence of a "golden rule" makes conflict over voting rules inevitable.

You may be somewhat uneasy about describing politics as a kind of battle or contest, where people work to stack the deck in favor of alternatives they prefer. You may want politics to be about a search for what's good or fair. These are noble sentiments, but they do not reflect what happens in the real world. The American political process is indeed a contest, one marked by conflicts over what government should do and conflicts over how these choices should be made. To ignore these behaviors is to misunderstand what American politics is all about.

A second response to this complaint comes from the Reverend Charles L. Dodgson, a mathematician and voting scholar in the 1800s.[12] The Royal Academy in Britain had given Dodgson the task of devising a fair scheme of voting to be used in the election of Academy members.

Dodgson concluded, as this chapter does, that different voting rules can produce different results, and that no method is obviously better than all others. He conceded that the ability to manipulate

---

[12]Reverend Dodgson is better known as Lewis Carroll, the author of *Alice in Wonderland*. Dodgson's work on voting rules apparently influenced at least one scene in the book. The book describes a footrace that resembles a voting cycle: one runner is faster than the second, and the second faster than the third, but the third is faster than the first. For details, see William H. Riker, *The Art of Political Manipulation* (New Haven: Yale University Press, 1986), chapter 10.

outcomes by changing the rules might reduce an election to a game of skill rather than being a way to measure what people want. The solution, he argued, was not to condemn manipulation or devise methods of voting in which manipulation was impossible. Rather, Dodgson argued, people should be educated about rules and sophisticated behavior, in order to ensure, "that all shall know the rules by which the game may be won."[13]

This book follows Dodgson's advice. The goal here is to understand strategic behavior, regarding both the choice of rules and the institutions those rules produce. With this information in hand, you will be in a better position to understand why things happen in American politics and better able to pursue your own goals.

---

[13]Quoted in William H. Riker, *The Art of Political Manipulation* (New Haven: Yale University Press, 1986), p. 32.

_3_

Cooperation in Politics

C ooperation is fundamental to politics. Winning an election, writing and enacting legislation, influencing agency bureaucrats,
and virtually any other political activity usually involves first getting
people to act together in pursuit of common goals.

One kind of cooperative behavior in politics involves the formation
of interest groups, like the National Rifle Association (NRA) or the
American Association of Retired Persons (AARP). Cooperation here
involves convincing people to join the organization. Given enough
members and their dues, these groups can hire lobbyists, publicize
their issue agenda, and work to elect candidates who agree with
them.

A similar but distinct kind of cooperation involves political deals,
agreements, and bargains. A good example is vote trading, or
"logrolling," where one group of House members helps enact a proposal favored by another group in return for similar efforts in favor of
a proposal that the first group prefers. Here cooperation entails carrying out your end of the bargain—voting as the trade requires or
writing a proposal as you have agreed to.

This chapter focuses on cooperation in American politics and on a
deceptively simple question: Who cooperates? When do ordinary cit-

izens donate their time or money to an interest group or political party? When do members of Congress work together?

In both cases, cooperation is not automatic. Potential members of an interest group would rather sit back and let others pay their share of the costs. Members of Congress prefer to watch their colleagues implement their end of a deal, then renege when it is their own turn. But if no one cooperates, nothing is accomplished and everyone will be worse off. Thus the question: What institutions or other mechanisms give rational actors the incentive to cooperate?

Along with two distinct kinds of cooperation, this chapter presents two descriptions of how rational actors can be persuaded to ignore the incentives against cooperation. One solution, the theory of *collective action*, focuses on the decision to contribute to a joint enterprise, such as an interest group.[1] This solution emphasizes both how institutions allow groups to coerce people into cooperating and how institutions allow groups to provide additional benefits to people who join.

The second solution, the theory of *the shadow of the future*, addresses the decision to carry out a bargain or deal among rational actors. Here cooperation can be achieved if it involves repeated interactions rather than just one and if institutions allow people to monitor each other's compliance with the bargain.[2]

Both of these theories assume that people are rational actors who will cooperate only when it serves their interests. In particular, the fact that everyone wants cooperation to occur is not enough to ensure that it happens. Rather, cooperation occurs only given the right rules and institutions, such as those that coerce cooperation, deliver an extra benefit to participants, and facilitate monitoring.

The Logic of Collective Action

To illustrate the problem of collective action, consider a group of senior citizens who want to lobby their town to establish a free shuttle-van service that will stop at seniors' homes and take them shopping once a week.

---

[1]This discussion will be drawn from Mancur Olson, *The Logic of Collective Action* (Cambridge, Mass.: Harvard University Press), 1966.
[2]This theory is from Robert Axelrod, *The Evolution of Cooperation* (New York: Basic Books, 1984).

Assume that all seniors in the community want this service, and all are willing to do their share of lobbying and related work (e.g., attend meetings, develop cost estimates, plan routes, etc.). Assume further that these seniors are rational actors, who know the benefits of a shuttle service and the costs involved with lobbying and that they are sure that these benefits exceed the costs. Finally, assume that the town council is sure to approve a shuttle proposal if seniors lobby for it. Will lobbying occur?

The answer is, surprisingly, probably not. While each senior wants the shuttle van, each has an opportunity to *free ride*—get the benefit of cooperation (the shuttle service) without paying the cost (lobbying). After all, the van will stop at everyone's house, regardless of whether the occupant lobbied. Accordingly, a rational senior might say something like "I really want that van service. The council will approve the proposal only if most of the other seniors in town show up to the council meeting and speak out. Either most will go, and my individual efforts won't make a difference, or most won't, and my effort will be wasted. Either way, my staying home won't matter. Thus, even though I want the service, my rational choice is to stay home and watch *Buffy the Vampire Slayer* instead."

But what happens if every senior makes this rational calculation? No one will show up at the meeting, and council members, believing that no one wants a shuttle service, will vote the proposal down.

At first glance, these seniors are behaving irrationally: Each wants the shuttle service, but none is willing to invest the time needed to make it happen. Why do they refuse to take actions that are mutually beneficial?

Want a real example? Think about yourselves. Most college students believe that the federal government should provide generous student-aid packages, low interest rates for student loans, and other subsidies that help people pay for higher education. However, despite their common interests and the fact that government could do more to help students, college students are among the most unorganized groups in American politics. There have been many attempts to organize an interest group for college students, but none have been successful.

A Web search in November 1999 for student organizations produced over two dozen hits, ranging from the National Association of Graduate-Professional Students to the American Podiatric Medicine Students Organization. A look at these organizations reveals that most have only a few members, and none do any significant lobbying, either for their members or for students broadly defined. The point is not that these organizations shouldn't exist; rather, the point is that none are organized to lobby for the things students want. Absent such a group, members of Congress have no reason to take account of students' demands.

The fact that groups of like-minded people fail to organize to lobby government contradicts how most of us think democracy should work. Most people would say that interest drives organization. That is, once people recognize that they want the same things from government, they will easily and automatically band together and work to achieve their common goals, writing letters, organizing public protests, talking to congressional staff and bureaucrats, working for candidates, and making campaign contributions.

This expectation is plausible precisely because it is consistent with how many interest groups operate. Consider the NRA, an organization whose official history describes it as "America's foremost defender of Second Amendment rights."[3] The NRA has some three million members. The organization operates over 150 programs designed to promote gun safety, marksmanship, law enforcement, and gun ownership. Moreover, the NRA's lobbying budget is in the millions of dollars. NRA staff, including the organization's current president, the actor Charlton Heston, work to convince members of Congress that there is no need for additional regulations on firearms. The NRA also endorses candidates who agree with its positions and runs campaign ads to help them win and hold office.

However, not all groups of like-minded people have organizations that are as large and well financed as the NRA. Again, think about students. It doesn't take much thought to see that government could do more to help people get through college, or that legislators would listen carefully to a lobbyist from an organization that had millions of dues-paying college students as members. Yet, as the web search illustrates, there are no interest groups that fight for college students. Nor did such an organization form during opposition to the Vietnam War and the draft in the 1960s, or when massive cuts in student aid occurred in the early 1980s.

The fact that so many interests in society are latent or unorganized raises a simple question: Why do common interests lead to the formation of an interest group in some situations but not others? What factors explain this variation in organization?

[3]www.nrahq.org/history.shtml

A second question concerns choices about the goals of organized interest groups. Simply put, why are some groups dominated by their leaders—to the point that the policies these groups lobby for are contrary to the interests of the membership? Intuitively, leaders should want the same things as the members or, when disagreements arise, behave as group members prefer. Yet there are many examples of interest groups lobbying for policies that their members oppose.

For example, in 1988 the AARP lobbied for a program that would help senior citizens pay for long-term hospital stays. After the program was enacted, it became clear that seniors did not favor the scheme. On the contrary, they were strongly against it. What explained the AARP's official position? The leadership of the organization apparently disregarded their members' preferences in favor of their own. (Additional discussion of this example will appear later in this chapter.)

The next section explains why some interests are unrepresented. As you will see, individuals who are in full agreement with an interest group's mission may nonetheless decide against helping the group achieve these goals. The reason is not that individuals are irrational, stupid, or venal, or because the cost of cooperating is too high. The difficulty lies with the nature of the benefits supplied by the group. Would-be organizers must devise a solution to their free-rider problem. That is, they must develop institutional solutions that change the incentives facing would-be free riders. Some groups are advantaged because institutions exist that allow them to coerce members. Others have or can develop selective incentives to induce cooperation. And some groups find that members join because they value participation. Without these solutions the group is likely to remain inactive or unorganized, even if cooperation would be enormously beneficial.

Cooperation in Large Groups: A Hypothetical Example

To see why cooperation in large groups can be problematic, imagine the following scenario. A group of people can make themselves better off by cooperating. Each member of the group has two choices, cooperate or "defect" (to use the standard term for an individual's refusal to cooperate). Cooperating produces benefits for all group members but also requires an individual to incur some cost. An individual who defects receives his share of the benefits produced if other group members cooperate but incurs no cost himself.

This scenario matches the earlier description of the senior shuttle-van service; it illustrates as well the situation of college students. Students could influence government policy by lobbying. However, lobbying requires organization, and an organization requires students to cooperate—at a minimum, to join the organization as a dues-paying member.

Suppose someone tries to create a new interest group for students, Students Allied for Policy Shifts, or SAPS. If enough students join SAPS, it will have funds to open a Washington office, hire lobbying staff, run newspaper and television ads, and do all the other things that help convince members of Congress to respond to its demands.

Besides cooperating, each student has a second choice: Defect, or refuse to join SAPS. A defecting student saves whatever dues she would pay to SAPS. However, if SAPS succeeds in raising Pell grants and lowering student loan rates, these benefits are shared by *all* students—all defectors get the larger grant and the lower rates and save paying dues.

Finally, assume that the benefits that a student would receive if SAPS is successful outweighs the individual's dues payment. That is, the amount of money a student would gain from higher Pell grants and lower loan rates exceeds whatever dues he would pay to join SAPS. This assumption makes sense. An increase in Pell grants would likely be in the hundreds of dollars, and even a small decrease in interest rates would save the average student thousands of dollars in future payments. Set against the twenty or so dollars in annual dues payments, these benefits are quite substantial.

Given these benefit and cost assumptions, a large, vibrant SAPS with many members would seem to be inevitable. However, as the next section shows, this is not in fact a situation where you should expect a lot of cooperation.

Public Goods. To understand why SAPS is doomed to fail, you must first consider the nature of the benefits that this organization aims to create. Changes in government policy are *public goods.*[4] That is, if the government increases Pell grants, everyone who is eligible receives the increase. There's no way to exclude people based

---

[4]The "good" in public goods refers to the fact that public goods are tangible commodities; it has nothing to do with an individual's evaluation of the commodity. Thus, supplying a public good to someone may make him worse off. The "public" part signifies that once the good is supplied to one person, everyone get it. Policy changes are public goods, while the CDs you buy at a music store are not.

on whether they helped to create this change, such as by joining SAPS.

The nature of public goods is critical for explaining why people would refuse to join a group like SAPS. If exclusion were possible, the benefits of SAPS's lobbying could be restricted to those individuals who helped create this change—people who joined the organization. People who abstained wouldn't receive anything. When exclusion is impossible, as in the case of SAPS, benefits must be supplied to cooperators and defectors alike. As a result, would-be defectors can *free ride*, or refuse to join, knowing that if lobbying succeeds, they will benefit, even though they refused to help.

The second reason for SAPS's failure is that cooperation is voluntary. Representatives from SAPS can send letters asking students to join, they can call late at night, or send thousands of E-mails. However, these representatives can't force anyone to send in their dues. If a student ignores these messages, there's nothing that SAPS can do to change her mind.

While each of these problems seems surmountable by itself, taken together they generate a situation where it is extremely difficult to form an interest group. Consider the perspective of Joe Doe, student at the State University of New York at Stony Brook.[5] It costs Doe something to join SAPS, money that could be spent on books, school supplies, or approved nonalcoholic beverages. Moreover, Doe's individual cooperation won't have much effect on the success or failure of SAPS's lobbying efforts. In order to have the funds and the membership to influence Congress, millions of students need to join SAPS. Measured in these terms, Doe's dues wouldn't even be a drop in the bucket.

This logic suggests that Doe should refuse to join SAPS. Doe might reason as follows:

- "Suppose lots of students join SAPS. Then the organization has everything it needs to influence Congress, and there's no need for me to join. I would do better by spending my dues elsewhere and simply enjoying the benefits of SAPS's success."
- "Suppose only some students join SAPS—enough to fund some lobbying, but not enough to ensure success. Here again, I do better by refusing to join. Having one additional member is not likely

[5]For the record, the author's undergraduate degree is from Stony Brook, class of 1982.

to help all that much. Refusing to join saves me some dues and doesn't reduce the chances that my Pell grant will be increased or my loan rates reduced."

• "Suppose SAPS attracts only a few members. Then the organization is sure to fail, and any dues I pay will be wasted."

The point is simple. Regardless of whether Doe expects a lot, some, or only a few students to join SAPS, his optimal strategy is to free ride.

While Doe is only one potential member, every student faces the same calculation. In other words, each potential SAPS member sees free riding as an optimal strategy. But if everyone follows up on this calculation, no one will join SAPS, and the organization will be unable to lobby for pro-student policies.

This example also demonstrates how rational calculations may not produce optimal results. When all students free ride, no lobbying occurs. However, remember that I've assumed that the benefits of successful lobbying outweigh the costs of joining SAPS. In other words, all students would prefer a situation where everyone joined SAPS (and lobbying succeeded) to one where everyone free rides (and no lobbying occurs). The problem is that each student's rational calculation leads her away from the all-join outcome and toward a free-ride outcome (although there won't be anything to free ride on).

The Free Rider Problem. The SAPS example illustrates a general point: Common interests are not enough to ensure cooperation. When the benefits of cooperation are public goods, individuals face an incentive to free ride. For each individual, free riding eliminates the cost of cooperating while reducing potential benefits only slightly. However, if everyone free rides, no benefits will be produced. Collective action will not occur, despite the fact that everyone prefers the outcome produced by universal cooperation over that produced by universal defection.

In real-world terms, the free-rider problem implies that you should not expect that people who want the same things from government will necessarily organize to get it. Success hinges on whether these groups can solve the free-rider problem. Possible solutions will be discussed shortly. For now, it is important to understand that this logic explains why some groups remain inactive, despite the fact that members of the group would all be better off if they organized.

The logic of the free-rider decision also suggests a different interpretation of what it means when a group has no organized association to fight for its interests. Suppose you find that student's interests are unrepresented in Washington. One interpretation is that students all want different things; another is that they don't care enough to invest in organization. However, a lack of organization doesn't mean people disagree or that they don't care. It's just as likely that students know they can make themselves better off by forming an interest group but cannot solve their free-rider problem.

Solving Collective Action Problems

How do groups solve their collective action problem? Some of the time, they don't. Society is full of like-minded people (e.g., students) who are unable to organize. Even so, there are ways to solve this problem. This section discusses three factors that increase the likelihood of cooperation: benefits from participation, coercion, and selective incentives.

Benefits from Participation. Sometimes people receive benefits from participating in a group effort. Studies of political parties and interest groups find that some individuals volunteer for these organizations out of a desire to be among people who want the same things they do. This participation benefit has nothing to do with public goods; it is an intangible reward people receive simply by getting involved.

The Christian Coalition is a good example of an organization that attracts workers by offering participation benefits. These workers help the Coalition distribute its voting guides to millions of people as they leave church on the Sunday before an election day. The handouts encourage people to vote and alert the reader to candidates that the Coalition supports.

The Coalition's workers aren't paid for their efforts. Why do they volunteer? It appears that these volunteers simply value their participation in the operations of the Coalition—they prefer to participate. This behavior is completely rational, even though the benefits of participation are abstract rather than tangible. The act of getting involved makes these volunteers better off, regardless of whether their efforts have any impact on election returns.

If participation benefits were common, the free-rider problem would be a less serious obstacle to group formation. However, the fact that so many interests in contemporary American society are un-

organized suggests that only a small number of people derive participation benefits.

Coercion. A second way to solve the free-rider problem is through
institutions that force people to cooperate. Labor unions are a good
example. Unions provide public goods to workers in a particular fac-
tory or industry—they negotiate with management over pay and
work requirements. Workers cooperate when they join the union and
pay dues. But since a worker receives the benefit of the union's efforts regardless of whether or not they join, why not refuse and free
ride on the contributions of others?

The solution to this free-rider problem is simple. In the main, people join unions because membership is a condition of their employment.[6] This requirement is referred to as a *union shop* law. As first
glance, such laws appear to be quite unfair, as they force people to
join a union even if they disagree with the union's negotiating strategy or other actions. However, union shop laws are critical to the organization and preservation of unions. States with *right-to-work* laws,
the opposite of union shop laws, typically have weak or nonexistent
unions. This is no surprise. Right to work laws allow people to free
ride on a union's efforts to get better pay and working conditions.
The result, not surprisingly, is that unions are much less likely to
form or prosper in states where membership is an option rather than
a requirement.

Coercion is also used to motivate participation in professional organizations, such as local medical societies and the legal bar. In many
states, would-be doctors must join the local medical society (and pay
dues) in order to practice medicine. Membership in the state or local
bar is often a requirement for working as a lawyer. If doctors and
lawyers were not required to join their local professional organization, it is likely that far fewer would join and fewer of these organizations would exist—unless, of course, the organizations could find
another way to engender cooperation.

Selective Incentives. The use of *selective incentives* to reduce free riding is in many ways the most interesting remedy to this problem. Or-

---

[6]Some states allow individuals to decide against joining a union, as long as they agree
to pay the same dues as their colleagues. In other words, unions don't force workers
to join, but they have successfully lobbied for laws that require workers to support
the union's efforts with dues payments, even if they don't want to become a union
member.

ganizations provide these benefits in order to give potential members a reason to join. Selective benefits are not public goods: An individual receives the package of selective incentives only if she cooperates. Thus, selective incentives work against the free-rider problem. With these incentives in place, cooperation is still costly, but comes with a new benefit, one that is received only by cooperators. While a free rider will still reap any public-goods benefits the group successfully lobbies for, she will lose out on the selective incentives.

Many interest groups and political parties use selective incentives to motivate participation. Consider the NRA. Its Web site argues that "The most important benefit of NRA membership . . . is the defense of your Constitutional right to keep and bear arms." But in case that benefit is not enough to get you to join, consider the selective incentives provided to members:

- a subscription to *American Rifleman, American Hunter,* or *American Guardian*
- insurance for loss of firearms, as well as accidental death and dismemberment insurance
- discounts on airline tickets, hotel rooms, rental cars, household movers, home mortgages, laser vision correction, student loans, and checks with the NRA logo

Incentives

Clearly, these benefits cost the NRA something to provide. In that sense, they draw funds away from the NRA's primary mission of protecting the rights of gun owners. It must be that these benefits are necessary to sustain the NRA's membership.

Perhaps the most interesting example of selective incentives is the Automobile Association of America (AAA). Most people see AAA as an organization that provides emergency road service to its members. A member whose car breaks down can call AAA at any time, day or night, and the organization will dispatch a tow truck and driver. AAA also provides annotated maps and travel guides to its members, a travel agency, and a car-buying service. These and other services are described in detail in AAA's membership literature, whose cover declares in bold letters that "it pays to join."

There is no doubt that AAA members receive valuable services in return for their membership fee. However, these services mask the interest-group role of the organization. Representatives of AAA lobby government to enact many different kinds of policies. For example, in past years AAA has supported anti–drunk-driving legislation, such as police checkpoints and laws to prevent teenagers from driving under the influence. Moreover, AAA lobbies for road-building programs at the expense of other mass-transit initiatives, such as light-rail systems and bus networks.

In short, AAA looks like a provider of services. However, these services are in fact selective incentives designed to motivate people to join the organization. With membership fees in hand, AAA can provide these selective incentives—but its lobbying efforts also provide collective benefits in the form of changes in government policies.

Unlike the case of the NRA, few AAA members are aware of the group's efforts to shape what government does. They join AAA to receive towing services and free maps. These inducements function as selective incentives. They give individuals a new reason to join AAA, benefits that they receive only by joining the organization. The fact that AAA provides these benefits does not change the fact that it operates as an interest group. These selective incentives make collective action possible.

Collective Action Problems: A Summary. Could SAPS use one of these solutions to solve the free-rider problem and get students to join? Since SAPS as described here is a national organization with no local chapters, few students will see substantial participation benefits. And it's hard to imagine how SAPS could coerce people to join the organization. Selective incentives, then, appear to be the most useful tactic. Students might be enticed to join in order to receive coffee mugs with the SAPS logo, low-interest credit cards, cheap travel during spring break, or sweatshirts proclaiming their contribution to SAPS.

In other words, for SAPS to be successful, its staff must be more than experts at lobbying. They also have to give potential members a reason to join the organization. Coffee mugs, sweatshirts, and charter flights to Florida and Cancun may seem incompatible with the goal of shaping government policy. However, because of the free-rider problem, these selective incentives may be crucial for the group's success.

The Biases in Group Organization

Groups that provide benefits from participation, coercion, or selective incentives will find it easier to organize. Groups lacking these provisions are much less likely to organize—not because collective action isn't worthwhile, or because the benefits are overlooked, but because would-be members will try to free ride.

Thus, the set of organized interest groups that you observe is unlikely to reflect the entire range of interests in society. Organization will be biased in favor of groups that can solve their collective action problem. Because these groups are more likely to organize, they are also more likely to get what they want from government—not because their leaders are expert negotiators, or because the group is large or powerful, but because of rules and institutions that help them to organize in the first place.

Political Machines: An Example of a Solution. A good example of how collective action problems influence the propensity to organize comes from an examination of political machines.[7] Political machines are party organizations whose members are uninterested in policy, but try to gain control of government in order to provide benefits (services, jobs, and government contracts) to party workers and other individuals who support the party. Machines were active and quite successful in most urban areas of the United States at the beginning of the twentieth century. Some machines persist to this day—for example, the Democratic Party in Chicago and, until the 1999 election, the Republican Party in Nassau County outside New York City.

The interesting thing about political machines was their consistent ability to out-organize "good government" groups that wanted to end the practice of rewarding party workers. Up until the 1930s, good-government groups were unable to defeat the machines. The typical "goo-goo" organization lasted for only a few years and won no elections.

The logic of free riding helps to explain how the machines won. Political machines stressed the provision of selective incentives to party workers, contributors, and voters. Thus, machines had an easy time of organizing. Good government groups, in contrast, had policy platforms that amounted to public goods—an efficient government in which policies were chosen by objective criteria.

The problem is, advocates of good government could free ride on the efforts of others to provide it. As a result, good government groups had trouble getting people to work in their campaigns. The reformers could not use selective incentives to entice workers, for this strategy would contradict their reason for being. As a result, reform

[7]William L. Riordan, *Plunkett of Tammany Hall* (New York: E. P. Dutton, 1963).

organizations in the early part of the twentieth century were almost always short-lived and rarely were a serious challenge to political machines.

The example of political machines also demonstrates that changes in the supply of selective incentives can have profound implications for cooperation. Certainly there are fewer machines in the modern era than there were in the early twentieth century. Where did the machines go—why did they weaken and disappear? One critical factor was the imposition of civil service reforms that implemented a testing system for municipal employment. Under this system, applicants for a position had to take a test that measured their ability to do the job. People would be hired only if they received a sufficiently high score on the test. A second factor was that the Great Depression reduced the number of government jobs and other largesse that machines could distribute.

Civil service reforms and the high unemployment rate of the Depression eliminated a critical selective incentive for the machine: their ability to provide jobs. Without this incentive, machines could not attract the workers needed to do the mundane activities of campaigning, such as putting up posters, registering voters, and getting people to the polls. As a result, their ability to contest elections and thereby stay in power waned.

Why Leaders Call the Shots. Attracting members with selective incentives can lead to a situation where an interest group's lobbying agenda has nothing to do with the goals held by group's members. Intuitively, there should be a strong connection between what members want and what the group does—after all, why would people join an interest group that favored policies they opposed? However, when coercion or selective incentives drive membership, there is no necessary connection between member goals and group agendas.

Consider AAA. People join for the selective incentives—emergency road service, free maps, and discount travel. Few members know that AAA also functions as an interest group. Most wouldn't care if they found out.

The incentives facing people at the top of AAA are quite different. AAA's leaders get to decide which policies to lobby for and against. Because members only worry about the selective incentives, these lobbying decisions can be made independent of the goals and interests held by the members.

In short, what does AAA lobby for? What its leaders prefer. Are

AAA's lobbying efforts compatible with the interests of AAA members? Only if its members happen to favor the policies supported by the group's leaders.

While AAA may seem an exceptional case, the same sort of situation can arise for any interest group that uses selective incentives or coercion to motivate participation. You might expect that members of an interest group would quit or protest if their leaders did something completely outlandish. For example, if AAA began to lobby for restrictions on abortion or higher defense spending, some people would decide to get their road service elsewhere. However, as long as the leaders of an interest group take care to keep their lobbying quiet and not too extreme, they have enormous discretion over the positions their group supports.

A similar situation arises for labor unions. Unions provide public goods to their members in the form of collective bargaining services. Most unions also lobby government in favor of certain policies, and donate services and some cash to candidates who are expected to support these policies.

Do union members determine the union's lobbying strategy or its electoral decisions? Are members aware of the extent of their union's lobbying efforts? Do they get a say in who receives campaign contributions from the union—contributions paid for by their dues? The answer to all of these questions is no. A union's leadership decides which candidates to support. Union members are along for the ride, coerced into paying for lobbying and campaign contributions that they do not control and might not want.

Shifts in What Groups Do. The example of AAA shows how an interest group can look like a provider of selective incentives, with its political role hidden from most members. The ever-present danger to the interest group is that the provision of selective incentives may crowd out lobbying activities. That is, the leaders of a group may spend most of their time attracting and keeping members rather than trying to influence the policy process—the thing that the group organized to do in the first place.

The problem of interest groups mutating into service organizations is especially acute when groups compete for members. Consider senior citizen groups, where the competition is especially keen. No sooner does one group devise a new selective incentive, such as discounted hotel rates, then another group adds this benefit to its package. This competition reinforces the perception of these groups as service providers, and masks—or even undermines—their role as lobbying organizations.

Organized groups may also wind up supporting certain policies simply because of the selective incentives they allow the group to provide. For example, it appears that the AARP supported catastrophic health insurance because the program would subsidize drug prescriptions for senior citizens. While this change would provide a useful benefit to AARP members, it would also enhance one of the selective incentives that AARP provides to its members—a mail-order service that fills prescriptions at discounted rates.

The members of AARP did not ask their leaders to lobby for the drug benefit. Nor, apparently, did the leaders of AARP hold policy goals that would lead them to favor the drug benefit. Rather, the leaders' support for catastrophic insurance appears to have arisen (at least in part) from their interest in providing selective incentives to their members.

Groups Without Members. The logic of collective action also explains a seeming anomaly in real-world interest groups: Some groups have no members. Intuitively, organization reflects interests: The fact that a group comes into being suggests that there are some number of people in society who agree with the group's mission. However, the problem of overcoming the free-rider problem leads some groups to abandon the idea of membership entirely. These groups receive their funding from industry groups or from foundations. They claim to represent the interests of certain people or groups in society, but do not ask these people to join their organization or otherwise contribute to its operations.

An example of a group without members is the Coalition for Air Travel (CTA). This group, formed in the late 1980s, allegedly represents people who are frequent airline travelers. The CTA lobbies for improved air traffic control systems, new airports, and tighter safety regulations. However, the CTA was actually the creation of major airlines, which fund its operations and supply its staff. Its membership is generated by soliciting people who belong to one or more frequent flyer programs. These "members" pay no dues and have no role in the organization. Thus, while the Coalition looks like a mass interest group, it is in fact a creature of the airline industry.

Why do the major airlines fund the CTA? Presumably this organization gives them an indirect way to lobby for policy changes that would increase their profits. If, for example, the chief executive officer of American Airlines announced that he favored legislation that restricted the number of new airlines that could form, most people would see this proposal as a self-serving effort to limit competition. But suppose the CTA makes the same proposal, and justifies it by claiming it would prevent fly-by-night operators from getting into the airline business. Most people would probably accept the CTA's claim that it represents frequent travelers without any scrutiny and therefore be relatively sympathetic to the proposal.

Making the Deal Stick: Cooperation and the Shadow of the Future

This section focuses on cooperation that takes the form of bargains or deals, such as *vote trading*.[8] Cooperation in these situations typically requires each participant to take actions she would prefer to avoid in return for helpful actions taken by other parties to the deal. Thus the question: Under what circumstances are these deals carried out, given that each participant would prefer to renege on their part of the agreement?

A prime example of what this section considers is a vote trade that occurred in the U.S. Congress in October 1991—the "corn for porn" trade.[9] Senator Jesse Helms had sponsored a measure that would forbid the National Endowment for the Arts (NEA) from funding projects defined as obscene. A majority of the Senate had voted for Helms's proposal, but many liberal Democrats and moderate Republicans opposed the measure.

What did opponents of the restrictions do? They cut a deal. They promised to vote against a proposed increase in grazing fees paid by farmers in western states, a measure that most of them favored. In return, conservative western senators agreed to vote to undo the NEA restrictions.

After the deal was carried out and the NEA restrictions removed, Senator Helms accused his colleagues of "backroom deals and parliamentary flimflam," noting that, ". . . this is the first time an amend-

---

[8]Similar behavior occurs among bureaucrats, or between the president and members of Congress. And outside politics, businesses can conspire to fix prices or concede one market in return for dominance in another.
[9]For details, see "Restrictions on Grants Defeated," *New York Times*, November 1, 1999, p. C11.

ment I have offered has been defeated by a bunch of bull."[10] Even so, the compromise became law.

While the corn for porn trade was successful, the success of these bargains requires a solution to a fundamental problem: ensuring that each participant carries out his end of the deal. Opponents of the NEA restrictions had to vote against a proposal they favored in order to get the support needed to kill Helms's proposal. And legislators who opposed increased grazing fees needed to vote to save the NEA in order to get what they wanted. Both groups carried out their commitments. The question is, why?

This question extends well beyond explaining how legislators manage to trade votes. Any time cooperation takes the form of a deal, participants will be tempted to try to get something for nothing—to renege on their commitment, while reaping the benefits of cooperation by others. This problem will be illustrated here using the *prisoners' dilemma*, a description of a situation where two individuals can make each other better off by cooperating, but each faces a temptation to renege on any bargain they make.

The Prisoners' Dilemma

The prisoners' dilemma gets its name from the following situation.[11] Two individuals, Crusher and Masher, are arrested on suspicion of having committed some serious crime. Upon arriving at the police station, they are questioned in separate rooms.

The problem for the police is that, while they are confident that the suspects are guilty, they lack the evidence to prove this in court. The suspects know about this problem and also know that if they both remain silent, they will at worst be charged with some minor offense—disturbing the peace or driving with a broken taillight.

In an attempt to break the deadlock, the police offer each suspect a deal. Confess and implicate your partner, each suspect is told, and you will be released outright. If, however, you remain silent and your partner talks, you will be convicted for sure and receive a long prison term. If you both confess, you will both be convicted but receive a moderate sentence.

Each suspect now faces a difficult choice. If they both remain silent, they will each receive a small penalty. However, each suspect

[10]"Restrictions on Grants Defeated," p. C11.
[11]Axelrod 1984 contains a good discussion of the history of this game and how scholars have used it to explain political phenomena.

does better by confessing and implicating his partner, regardless of what his partner does:

- If Crusher expects his partner Masher to remain silent, Crusher does better by implicating Masher. This choice allows Crusher to avoid prison entirely, while silence gives him a short prison term.
- If Crusher believes that Masher will talk, then Crusher again does better by talking. This choice yields a moderate prison sentence, versus a longer sentence if Crusher remains silent in the face of his partner's decision.

These same options apply to Masher. The "dilemma" facing the two suspects is that if both follow this logic and implicate each other, they will receive moderate prison terms—a worse outcome than the short prison sentence they receive if both remain silent.

To see the problem another way, look at Figure 3.1, which shows the sentences given to each suspect depending on his strategy.

FIGURE 3.1
The Prisoners' Dilemma

		Masher's Choice	
		Remain Silent (Cooperate)	Implicate (Defect)
Crusher's Choice	Remain Silent (Cooperate)	Crusher: Short Sentence / Masher: Short Sentence	Crusher: Long Sentence / Masher: No Prison Time
	Implicate (Defect)	Crusher: No Prison Time / Masher: Long Sentence	Crusher: Moderate Sentence / Masher: Moderate Sentence

In the figure, the choices available to Crusher are arranged in rows, while Masher's choices are arranged in columns. Each cell in Figure 3.1 shows the sentences that each suspect will receive given a possible pair of choices. For example, the top lefthand cell shows that when both suspects cooperate and remain silent, they each receive a short sentence.

Figure 3.1 shows that if a suspect wants to avoid a long prison term, she is always better off defecting. However, if she wants to *minimize* her sentence, she must also defect—unless she is dead certain that her partner will remain silent. And if she *is* certain, she will still defect because this will result in no prison for her.

Another way to think of the prisoners' dilemma is in terms of a deal. As the two suspects are arrested, one quickly says to the other, "Keep quiet and we'll both get off." While the suspects can secure a pretty good outcome by following through on this deal, each sees the possibility of doing better by breaking the deal and informing on his partner, thereby getting off free and dooming his partner to a long stay in prison.

This description of the prisoners' dilemma will be familiar to anyone who watches police shows on network TV. Shows like *NYPD Blue*, *Law and Order*, or *Homicide* frequently have episodes where two suspects are interrogated separately, with the goal of getting one to implicate the other. The message given to each suspect is always the same: We don't care who talks, but we're going to give a good deal to the first one who does and throw the book at whoever remains silent. Or as the detectives on *Law and Order* are fond of saying, "The train's leaving the station, and you want to be on board."

Keep the image from TV in your mind for a moment. While these programs are fiction and politicians are not suspects, understanding this situation tells you a lot about what happens when real-world politicians try to trade votes or make other deals.

To begin with, the reason why the suspects find it hard to cooperate is not that they are bad people, ignorant of their situation, motivated by anger, or bamboozled by wily detectives. The problem is that reneging is a rational choice. Defecting—implicating your partner rather than keeping your mouth shut—*always* results in a shorter prison sentence. Neither of the suspects in this example have "lawyered up" and exercised their right to legal representation. But if one did, her lawyer would almost surely advise her to take the deal.

The typical interrogation scene also highlights why defection is hard to prevent. The suspects cannot make binding promises about their behavior. They can't pinky swear, or seal their deal by saying, "cross my heart and hope to die." Rather, fulfilling their commitment to cooperate—that is, keep quiet—has to be in their self-interest *at the time the commitment must be carried out.*

Moreover, the suspects have no third party to help them enforce their agreement. There is, of course, no such thing as the Mafia, but if there were, it would be a great help to these suspects if they were members and thereby subject to the code of *omerta*.[12] Each would remain silent, knowing that he would be severely punished for talking—and knowing that the other suspect faces the same threat. With a Mafia or some other enforcer who values silence, there would be no dilemma. But since there is no Mafia, the two prisoners are on their own. Whoever talks can escape to some other town long before the other is out on parole.

What can the prisoners do? It seems inevitable that one or both of the suspects in the example will renege on their bargain and talk to the police. In other words, their deal will unravel, and they will be unable to reap the benefits of cooperation. Two famous economists once suggested, half joking, that there ought to be a law against these sort of situations. The suspects would no doubt agree, although the police are undoubtedly happy.

Even so, situations that resemble the prisoners' dilemma are very common in politics. Do legislators follow the suspects' lead and renege on their bargains? If they did, or were expected to, then there would not be much evidence of vote trades or other kinds of legislative bargains in Congress—no corn for porn. But most observers of Congress believe that bargaining is a way of life for most members of the House and Senate. To paraphrase Sam Rayburn, a famous Speaker of the House, members get along by going along. Why would rational actors carry out their commitments, or agree to them in the first place?

What factors persuade legislators and prisoners to keep their word? The answer lies in the institutions that structure their interactions. In particular, if individuals interact frequently and are able to monitor each other's behavior, cooperation is relatively easy to sustain. All legislators have to do is follow a strategy of refusing to bargain with anyone who has reneged on a deal in the past. This sort of strategy is especially effective in the modern Congress, where members typically have long careers and face many opportunities to cooperate.

As you will see, situations where people interact frequently are ripe for cooperation. Participants in a vote trade or other deal can follow a strategy of cooperating with their colleagues, so long as their col-

---

[12]You'll understand the reference if you're seen *The Godfather*. If not, the idea is that the penalties for implicating your partner (or, worse yet, implicating people higher in the organization) are extremely severe—death, in fact. Or they would be, if the Mafia actually existed.

leagues have faithfully carried out their end of past bargains. When people use this strategy—and there is evidence that House and Senate members do—the attractiveness of being able to make future bargains constrains rational actors to carry out their commitments.

Political Dilemmas

It is easy to find examples of political dilemmas. Some, like the "corn for porn" trade discussed earlier, are explicit bargains. Another explicit trade occurred when members of the House Ways and Means Committee were involved in the writing of the 1986 Tax Reform Act. A number of committee members favored retaining a tax deduction for interest paid on vacation-home mortgages. The committee chair, Dan Rostenkowski, convinced them to drop their proposal in return for his support for transition rules—special tax relief given to businesses or individuals in the districts represented by these legislators.[13]

More commonly, deals and bargains in Congress are implicit. Rather than an explicit trade, giving this in return for getting that, a House member or Senator does a favor for a colleague in return for similar help on an unspecified matter at some point in the future.

A well-publicized example of implicit bargaining occurred during the Senate impeachment trial of President Clinton in early 1999. Many accounts emphasized how the majority and minority leaders, Republican Trent Lott and Democrat Tom Daschle, worked together throughout the trial.[14]

Lott, who as majority leader can determine the Senate's schedule, ignored the demands of House Republicans for unlimited testimony and agreed to restrictions on the length of the trial. When Republican senators demanded that three witnesses be deposed, Lott modified their proposal to allow Daschle a veto over any additional depositions or live testimony.

Daschle, in turn, discouraged Senate Democrats from making partisan comments about the trial and did not use parliamentary maneu-

---

[13]For an account of the 1986 Tax Reform Act, see David E. Rosenbaum, 1999. "The Nation: Then and Now; How to Pass a Great Big Law." *New York Times*, February 28, 1999, sec 4, p. 4.
[14]See Art Pine, "Senate Trial Gave a Boost to GOP's Lott," *Los Angeles Times*, February 16, 1999, p. A1; and Frank Bruni, "The President's Trial; The Leaders, Lott and Daschle, Forge New Bond in a Partisan Crucible," *New York Times*, February 7, 1999, p. 38.

vers to delay or undo Lott's proposed schedule. The leaders also held joint news conferences and gave each other a heads-up before announcing their party's positions or tactics.

The arrangements between the two leaders were never formally set out. Lott didn't say to Daschle, "I'll limit the number of witnesses if you convince your colleagues to be quiet." Rather, the deal was informal, open-ended, and probably never stated explicitly—certainly not in public.

However, the fact that the bargain between Lott and Daschle was implicit doesn't make it any less real. Each leader gave up something to his counterpart and got something in return. Lott committed to a short trial with only a few witnesses. Daschle refrained from criticizing Lott or other Republicans and persuaded most Democrats to do the same.

All three of these cases—corn for porn, tax reform, and impeachment—highlight how legislators can cooperate to their mutual benefit. The question remains, why didn't these legislators, like the prisoners in the dilemma, renege or defect? Why, for example, did opponents of NEA restrictions carry out their half of the vote trade? Why didn't the members of Ways and Means propose amendments on the floor of the House to undo their deal with Rostenkowski? And why didn't Daschle let his colleagues criticize Trent Lott, after Lott had announced a schedule that gave Daschle what he wanted?

The point is simple: When you consider the prisoners' dilemma, it seems inevitable that these instances of cooperation in Congress should never have happened. Yet such cooperation is often observed. Why is it that rational actors are led away from cooperation in one situation and toward it in another? Or, to put it another way, what is different about the deals that legislators make that makes cooperation a rational choice?

When and Why Do Legislators Cooperate?

Why is cooperation a rational choice in Congress? The answer is simple: The institutions that structure deals in Congress differ from the classic prisoners' dilemma in one critical respect. In contrast to the two suspects, members of Congress interact more than once—they are in a *repeat play* situation. The picture in the prisoners' dilemma is of two career criminals who were arrested together but who have no lasting ties or relationship. The typical member of Congress, in contrast, stays in office for ten to twenty years. During this time, there are plenty of opportunities to make mutually beneficial deals with colleagues.

The fact that members of Congress interact repeatedly rather than once has a dramatic impact on their ability to reap the benefits of cooperation. Repeated interactions allow members to behave in ways that change the incentives available to the people they make deals with and thereby eliminate the temptation to renege.

Repeated Interactions. To say that individuals in Congress or elsewhere interact repeatedly means that circumstances allow them to make a number of deals or bargains in future weeks, months, and years. In terms of the prisoners' dilemma, it is as though the two suspects faced the same set of choices not once but a large number of times.

This description neatly describes the circumstances of congressional cooperation. Consider Trent Lott and Tom Daschle. The deals they made during President Clinton's impeachment trial were only a small fraction of a much larger set of interactions. Every day that the Senate is in session each leader is likely to be in a position to help the other. Daschle might need an early adjournment to allow Senate Democrats to attend a fundraiser or a vote on an amendment that is favored by the members of his caucus.[15] Lott, in turn, might want Daschle to prevent his colleagues from using their right of unlimited debate to delay a vote or to offer a compromise on the timing of budget votes. One reporter even claimed that Lott had given Daschle advance warning that a senior Republican Senator was going to announce his retirement.[16]

Will Lott always give Daschle what he wants or vice versa? Probably not. At least sometimes, a leader might ask for something that his counterpart is unwilling to give. Even so, the critical point is that opportunities for cooperation between the minority and majority leaders arise frequently. This statement holds even for average members of the House and Senate: They may not interact every day, but opportunities arise from time to time when one member can help another with a vote, some advice about hiring staff, or some other service.

That members of Congress interact repeatedly has a profound impact on their decisions about cooperation. To see the impact, imag-

---

[15]A caucus is an informal group of legislators who share common interests and political opinions.

[16]Ed Henry, "Heard on the Hill," *Roll Call Online*, November 8, 1999.

ine a situation where two legislators could make each other better off
by trading votes—say a new "corn for porn" trade. However, after
the NEA restrictions and grazing fees are voted on, each legislator
will retire from politics and return to her home town.

You wouldn't expect to see cooperation in this situation—indeed,
you probably wouldn't see much discussion about cooperation in the
first place. What's the problem? Each legislator knows that the person
whose favored proposal is voted on first will be in a perfect position
to renege.

Say the NEA restrictions come up first, followed by the grazing fee
bill.[17] Once supporters of the NEA get enough votes to kill the restrictions, they can vote for increased grazing fees, pack their bags,
and catch the next plane to Pawtucket. Opponents of increased grazing fees, who loyally voted against the NEA restrictions, will no
doubt be angry, but there is very little they can do.

The situation is quite different if the people involved in a vote
trade know that many other bargains are likely to come up in the future. In this situation, would-be defectors must consider a new question: How will reneging on the current deal affect the prospects for
future cooperation?

Consider the "corn for porn" trade and assume that grazing rights
are voted on second. If this is the only deal that will ever be made,
NEA supporters have a clear rational choice: renege. The situation is
different when the corn for porn trade is one of many. Now NEA
supporters must consider the long-term consequences of their behavior. If they refuse to carry out their end of the bargain, those senators
who helped them kill the NEA restrictions by trading votes may respond by refusing to make any future deals with them.

As this discussion suggests, repeat play is only part of the explanation for why legislators cooperate. The other part of the answer concerns how legislators respond to a colleague's failure to cooperate.
This response is discussed next.

Trigger Strategies. How do legislators get would-be defectors to
worry about the consequences of their behavior? By making future

---

[17]In fact, when the two proposals were voted on in 1992, they were bundled into a
single measure and voted on together. Even so, bundling doesn't make reneging impossible. After the combined measure passed, NEA supporters could have submitted
a new proposal that raised grazing fees, thereby undoing the half of the trade that
they didn't like.

cooperation with a colleague contingent on the colleague's past behavior. Such behavior is called a *trigger strategy*.

In its simplest form, a legislator following a trigger strategy behaves as follows:

- The first time you make a deal with a colleague, faithfully carry out your end of the bargain.
- After the first deal, never bargain with your colleague if he reneges.[18]

This trigger strategy promotes cooperation in two ways. First, a legislator who follows this strategy will never be the first to defect—she will always bargain in good faith and comply with the deals she makes.[19]

Second, trigger strategies impose significant costs on legislators who make deals but refuse to carry them out. If you employ a trigger strategy, a legislator who makes a deal with you knows that if he defects, you will never bargain with him again. Your strategy changes your colleague's calculation from, "I can do better by defecting, so I will," to "While I see some advantage to defecting, I must balance off these gains against the benefits I will lose when my opponent refuses to make any future bargains with me."

If you and your colleague interacted only once, this calculation wouldn't have much impact—why worry about the future when there isn't one. But if your colleague believes that there will be many opportunities to bargain with you in the future, then he is likely to decide against reneging on the current deal. Why? Because it would foreclose any chance of receiving benefits from future interactions.

To see the impact of trigger strategies on cooperation, recall the bargains made by Lott and Daschle. Each time one leader helped the other during the impeachment trial, he faced a decision: Should I co-

---

[18]Robert Axelrod argues that people should use a more forgiving strategy, where they resume bargaining with a defector after he has done them at least one favor without getting anything in return. The discussion here focuses on a more severe trigger strategy because it better fits how members of Congress actually behave.

[19]You may wonder why this half of the strategy is rational: Why start off cooperating when you might do better by defecting? Or, to put it another way, trigger strategies are good at eliminating your opponent's incentive to defect, but what about your own temptation? The answer is that for trigger strategies to be successful in creating cooperation, everyone (or almost everyone) has to use them. When everyone uses them, no one is tempted to renege.

operate or defect? The answer is easy. Lott and Daschle both expect
to be senators and leaders of their respective party caucuses for some
time to come. For these leaders, reneging on a deal doesn't make
much sense—if the other leader uses a trigger strategy, one act of
reneging could make all future deals impossible. Each legislator cooperates because he doesn't want to kill the goose that lays the
golden egg.

The combination of repeated interactions and trigger strategies
creates what Robert Axelrod calls the *shadow of the future.*[20] When
legislators (or any other group of rational actors) know that they will
meet again, and when they expect that reneging on a deal will cost
them a sizable number of future benefits, they will take care to carry
out the bargains they make. The shadow of the future doesn't turn
legislators into angels, ensure that they will agree to bargains in the
first place, or eliminate the cost of carrying out their commitments.
Rather, the shadow of the future forces legislators to consider the
consequences of their behavior. Defection is transformed from an
easy way to make yourself better off into a dangerous tactic that
could cost you a large number of future benefits.

Do Members of Congress Really Use Trigger Strategies? I'm sure that
if you asked a member of Congress about trigger strategies and the
shadow of the future, she would respond with a polite, blank stare
and a noncommittal response. But this reaction only means that the
legislator isn't up on the latest political science jargon. There's lots of
evidence that congressional behavior is based on some kind of trigger
strategy.

The rule in Congress seems to be that you don't have to make
deals, but you are expected to carry out the deals you make. Whether
you're a party leader, a committee chair, or a lowly first-term member, you can decide to opt out of the bargaining process without
penalty. The penalties arise only if you renege on a bargain. If you
do, legislators who were harmed by your defection will refuse to deal
with you in the future. Uninvolved legislators may refuse to deal with
you as well, on the grounds that you've demonstrated that you're not
a reliable partner.

And, lest you think that refusing to bargain is the only punishment
you would incur by reneging, consider the following examples, which
comes from Robert Caro's account of how one Speaker of the

---

[20]Axelrod, 1984.

House, Sam Rayburn, responded to a defection.[21] Rayburn ran the Democratic Caucus in the House on a kind of giant implicit bargain. Loyal caucus members received plum committee assignments, favorable treatment of proposals, and perks such as good office space. And if a member was defeated or retired, Rayburn would ensure that he was offered a good job in government or as a lobbyist. In return for Rayburn's largesse, caucus members were expected to help Rayburn whenever he asked, with votes and other small favors. The only exception was if doing so would reduce a member's political support back home. Then Rayburn would release the member from his obligation.

One day, Rayburn had asked a member to vote for a proposal that Rayburn wanted to enact. The member refused, arguing that his constituents would be angry. Rayburn, famous for his encyclopedic knowledge of American politics, knew that the member wasn't telling the truth—the political fallout would be minimal.

After a memorable public explosion of temper at the member's refusal to cooperate, Rayburn's punishment was swift and overwhelming. Caro tells how Rayburn was able to end this congressman's political career:[22]

> A young state legislator who had considered challenging the Congressman for his seat had dropped the idea because he didn't have enough political clout. Not a week after the confrontation with Rayburn, the Congressman walked into the House Dining Room for lunch and saw the [state] legislator sitting there—sitting at Rayburn's table. When the legislator returned home, he had all the clout he needed, and the Congressman's political career was over. Rayburn not only drove him out of Congress, but out of Washington. He tried to stay in the capitol, looking for a government job or a lobbying job, but no job was open to him. And none would ever be—not as long as Sam Rayburn was alive.

No wonder that legislators still repeat Rayburn's advice: "To get along, go along." They may not always make bargains, but they carry out the bargains they make. And their cooperation is driven by a thoroughly practical consideration, the expectation that defection will be punished.

Undoubtedly some members of Congress are honorable men and

---

[21]Robert A. Caro, *The Years of Lyndon Johnson: The Path to Power* (New York: Alfred A. Knopf, 1982). Chapter 18 describes Rayburn.
[22]Caro, p. 330.

women who would carry out their bargains even in a world where the shadow of the future was not a consideration. However, a sense of honor is not necessary for cooperation to succeed. Even when the temptation to defect exists and is strong, the prospect of future interactions, coupled with the use of trigger strategies, can ensure that members keep to the bargains they make.

Cooperation in Congress: A Summary

Legislators cooperate. They trade votes and other forms of assistance both explicitly and implicitly. The critical thing to remember is that their cooperation is not born of goodwill or indifference. For Trent Lott, Tom Daschle, and other members of Congress, cooperation is a rational response to the combination of institutions that ensure frequent, repeated interactions and members' use of trigger strategies to reward cooperation and punish defection.

This solution to the problem of enforcing deals in Congress is not surprising, because it mirrors how cooperation works outside the political arena. Why do people do favors for each other? In part, at least, because they expect favors in return. Roommates lend each other clothes, small sums of money, and Internet access; people in the same class trade texts, class notes, and, occasionally and unfortunately, cheat sheets; homeowners exchange power tools, babysitting, and assistance with moving heavy objects.

As in the case of Lott and Daschle, these trades are rarely explicit. But underneath this informality there is usually a clear expectation that cooperation will be reciprocated. Remember what *The Godfather*'s Don Corleone told his wayward friend after agreeing to help him: "Some day, and that day may never come, I'll call upon you to do a service for me. But until that day, accept this justice as a gift on my daughter's wedding day."

Most people agree with this sentiment. They are willing to help each other out but are unwilling to be exploited. They will refuse to deal with someone who doesn't respond to cooperation with cooperation. Sound sensible? Sound like how you try to behave? Congratulations. Like members of Congress, you try to ensure cooperation by using a trigger strategy.

Is Cooperation Really Easy? This section began with the claim that it's hard to get legislators to cooperate because they will be tempted to renege or defect. It ended by showing that rational actors can overcome this temptation if they interact frequently and use trigger strategies.

Am I arguing that cooperation is an easy thing to achieve, in Congress or elsewhere? The answer is no. Sometimes a failure to cooperate is a rational choice. Suppose Lott ask Daschle to abandon the Democratic agenda or roll over on budget negotiations. Complying with this request would be so costly for Daschle that there's no way he would see it as a good bargain, regardless of what Lott was expected to offer in return, either up front or over time. Thus, Daschle's refusal doesn't imply that he is unwilling to cooperate in general, but simply that Lott asked for too much.

In other situations, the shadow of the future may not exist. In politics and elsewhere, many people interact only once or only once in a while. Under these conditions, a threat of future punishment wouldn't be very effective. However, failure to cooperate doesn't imply that the participants don't appreciate the benefits of cooperation or that they aren't smart enough to use trigger strategies. Rather, it is a completely rational response to the nature of their interactions.

An example of the value of frequent interactions comes from Representative George Nethercutt, who won a House seat in 1994 in part because he promised to retire after three terms. By mid-1999, this pledge seemed less and less attractive to Representative Nethercutt, who announced that he planned to run for several more terms.[23] The reason? His promise to retire early limited his effectiveness in Washington—people wouldn't bargain with him.

That Nethercutt had trouble getting things done in Washington is no surprise. The problem was not his generally conservative agenda. Rather, other members of Congress were extremely reluctant to bargain with a colleague who had pledged to retire early, because the normal constraint on reneging, the shadow of the future, did not apply.

As of this writing, it is unclear whether Nethercutt will be reelected. Many people in his district are angry at his decision to abandon his pledge—one indication is that "George the Weasel King," a man in a weasel costume, shows up at many Nethercutt forums and appearances. Another is that the Democratic Party has targeted Nethercutt's seat as one they think they can win in 2000.

The voter's anger at Nethercutt for saying one thing and trying to

---

[23]Thomas B. Edsall, "Nethercutt Abandons Pledge to Serve Three Terms," *Washington Post*, June 15, 1999, p. A13.

do another is understandable. However, Nethercutt's change of heart illustrates one of the most important aspects of how Congress operates. The House and Senate are careerist institutions where the typical member stays in office for fifteen years or more. This situation is ripe for the emergence of cooperation based on the shadow of the future. Nethercutt may be a weasel for trying to abandon his pledge. But in doing so, he is admitting the value of being a career politician as an aid in making bargains with his colleagues.

Summary

Getting people to cooperate requires more than just showing them that cooperation would be mutually beneficial. In the case of people acting together in a group, achieving cooperation requires a solution to the free-rider problem, such as selective incentives, coercion, or participation benefits. When cooperation takes the form of trades or bargains in the absence of *omerta* or something similar, it must be secured by the shadow of the future.

Both the difficulty of getting people to cooperate and the usefulness of the solutions discussed here exist because people are rational, self-interested actors. Rational actors are interested in maximizing their return, which leads them to free ride or to renege on bargains if they can do so without consequences.

In both cases, the solution is institutions that make defection costly. In the case of free riding, for example, selective incentives increase the attractiveness of cooperation. And when rational actors bargain, the shadow of the future reduces the temptation to reneging by eliminating the possibility of future interactions.

The essential message of this chapter is that cooperation in politics or elsewhere is not inevitable. When these solutions to these disincentives exist or can be imposed, rational actors will generally respond by cooperating. When these solutions are unfeasible, the prospects for cooperation are bleak—not because people are dumb or overly emotional, but because they are all too good at assessing where their self-interest lies.

Voters and Vote Decisions

Elections are fundamental to democracy. They allow citizens to select officeholders and thereby determine who makes the laws, writes the regulations, and otherwise controls what government does. Without elections, citizens have, at best, indirect power over government action, hoping that officeholders with no reason to act in the interests of citizens will nevertheless do so.

This chapter considers elections from the perspective of a rational voter, focusing on two questions. First, should you vote? Second, if you decide to vote, how should you choose among the candidates running for office? These questions will be addressed using a running example, a hypothetical election where there is one office at stake, President of the United States, and two candidates, McBush and Gradley.[1]

These questions reflect two interesting challenges to the assumption that people make rational choices. For one thing, many people

---

[1]The names of these hypothetical candidates are combinations of the names of the principle Republican (George W. Bush and John McCain) and Democratic (Al Gore and Bill Bradley) candidates in the 2000 contest. If you think I'm trying to make fun of the candidates, remember that I could have used other combinations, such as Mush and Bore.

abstain from voting, even when they have a strong preference for one candidate over the other—they like McBush a lot more than Gradley or vice versa.

Abstention would be no surprise if a voter thought that the candidates running for office were equally attractive or unattractive ("McBush and Gradley are both jerks"), or if she saw elections as irrelevant ("No matter who wins, aliens from Planet Ten control everything"). But why do citizens abstain when they have strong preferences and believe that government will do different things depending on which candidate wins?

The second anomaly is that the average voter ignores much of the policy-relevant information sent to him by the candidates. He doesn't look at McBush's interactive policy presentation on the Web or watch Gradley's ninety-minute video after it arrives in the mail, and he ignores everything else these candidates do to educate him about their policy positions.

How does the average voter decide? She votes on the basis of factors that appear to be totally irrelevant to politics, such as a candidate's gender, race, ethnicity, and personal life. She votes for Gradley because he can dance the Macarena or consistently hit three-point shots, or favors McBush because of his war record or reputation as a college party animal.

At first glance, these behaviors are fundamentally incompatible with the assumption that people are rational. How can it be rational to abstain when you care about who wins? And why is it rational to choose a candidate because of his skin color, occupation, or age—or his social life in college?

This chapter shows that these contradictions are easily explained. Both abstention and a focus on personal characteristics are a rational response to the situation that voters face in real-world elections.

The first part of the chapter shows why it is rational to abstain from voting, even when you have a strong preference for one candidate over another. The problem is that a citizen's vote is one of many and has a microscopic impact on election outcomes. True, many people do vote. The analysis here shows that their decision must be driven by factors other than their interest in electing their preferred candidates.

The second part of the chapter explains why voters are likely to ignore a candidate's attempts to educate them about her issue positions. The reason for this seemingly irrational behavior is not that this information is too costly to acquire or too hard to make sense of.

The problem is that most of what candidates say in campaigns is "cheap talk"—there is no cost to misrepresenting the truth.

Since candidates can easily lie about their intentions, and since they have good reason to do so, it makes sense that rational voters discount and even ignore much of what candidates tell them. Moreover, the average voter's focus on appearances or personal life makes sense, because many of these factors are correlated with policy positions and cannot be misrepresented to enhance a candidate's attractiveness.

Why Do People Abstain? Why Do They Vote?

Most descriptions of American elections use "citizen" and "voter" interchangeably. However, the decision to vote is really a decision, one with two equally valid choices, voting and abstention. Even in a year where the presidency is up for grabs, many citizens abstain rather than vote.

This section analyzes voting as a rational choice. It shows that many widely held intuitions about voting are, in fact, dead wrong. For example,

- A citizen who thinks that Gradley is vastly preferable to McBush is no more likely to vote than one who thinks that the two candidates are equally desirable.
- A citizen who thinks that the race is very close—that either Gradley or McBush has a good chance of winning—is no more likely to vote than one who thinks that one of the two candidates is almost sure to win.

These findings do not imply that citizens are misinformed or inept. Rather, these behaviors are entirely consistent with the assumption that people are rational actors.

When do rational actors vote? As you will see, turnout decisions are sensitive to (affected by) the cost of voting—the cost of becoming informed and the cost of physically going to the polls and casting a vote. A citizen who knows she prefers McBush to Gradley and who lives next door to the polling station is more likely to vote than someone who doesn't know much about the candidates and who faces a long drive to the nearest place to vote.

More importantly, turnout is more likely for citizens who see voting as an obligation rather than a choice. People who feel this way benefit from the act of voting itself, as distinct from the benefit they receive when their preferred candidate wins. Such participation benefits have nothing do with a voter's feelings about who should win the election, which is intuitively assumed to be what motivates people to vote. Even so, these benefits are entirely consistent with the rational-actor assumption.

Why Vote: The Benefits and Costs of Voting

Suppose you must decide whether to vote in the McBush vs. Gradley race. You are a rational actor (or so I've assumed), so your decision depends on the benefits you get from voting and the cost of casting a vote. Specifically, you will vote if benefits outweigh costs and abstain otherwise.

The Costs of Voting. Voting is costly. In the first place, you have to learn about McBush and Gradley, and determine which one you prefer. One strategy that's relatively costly in terms of time, effort, and some money is to follow the campaign in the newspaper, read the candidates' platforms and issue papers, watch speeches and debates, and, lastly, think about what all these data mean.

Let's assume that you try to minimize the costs of voting. Accordingly, you don't do any research about the candidates. Rather, you listen to Rush Limbaugh or Howard Stern and vote for whoever they endorse.

Even if you follow this simple information-gathering strategy, it still costs something to vote. These are the costs associated with actually going to the polls and voting.

Think about your own situation. Most universities have a polling place that's near campus, so transportation costs are minimal. Accordingly, your principal cost is whatever value you place on the time it takes to vote. Casting a vote requires you to give up an hour or so when you could be working, studying, watching a soap opera, going to the gym, having coffee, or doing whatever you do in a normal day. It's hard to express that cost in monetary terms, but there's no doubt that it exists.

The Benefits from Voting. The first and most obvious benefit from voting is that it helps to elect your preferred candidate or candidates.[2]

---

[2]As discussed in Chapter 2, Americans vote for presidential electors rather than candidates, so it's not completely realistic to say that your vote (or anyone's vote) can break a tie and thereby cause one candidate to win. These details are ignored here in order to keep the example simple.

Your *differential*, or benefit of having your preferred candidate win, can be large or small depending on how you think the candidates will behave in office.

Imagine a situation where you think that Gradley will implement all the policies you favor—decrease taxes, increase defense spending, and offer subsidies for computer purchases by college students—while McBush will always do the opposite. In this case, your differential would be relatively large.

At the opposite extreme, suppose you agree with George Wallace that "there's not a dime's worth of difference" between Gradley and McBush, meaning that government policy will look the same regardless of who gets elected. If so, your differential is small.

Comparing Benefits and Costs: The Paradox of Voting. You may be thinking, Okay, so we've calculated the benefits and costs of voting, let's compare them and decide whether to vote or abstain. Not yet. The problem is that the differential, the benefit you receive when your preferred candidate wins, is not the same thing as the benefit you receive from voting. Why? Your decision to vote doesn't always determine whether you receive the differential. Suppose you prefer McBush to Gradley. If so, you receive the differential if McBush wins and nothing if Gradley does—regardless of whether you voted or abstained.

You may be thinking, wait a minute. Are you telling me that voting doesn't increase the chances that I get the differential, that it doesn't increase the chances that my preferred candidate wins? Almost. Your vote matters only in one situation: when you are *pivotal*, meaning the other voters split their votes evenly between Gradley and McBush and your vote breaks the tie. If you're not pivotal, the election will turn out the same way (Gradley will win or McBush will win) regardless of whether you vote or abstain.

In other words, you can't decide the benefit of voting only by comparing two variables: the differential and the cost of voting. You have to consider a third variable: the probability that you're the pivotal voter.

Confused? Here's an example. Suppose we play a game: I flip a coin, and give you two dollars if it comes up heads. (In other words, your benefit from heads, the differential, is two dollars.) It's a fair coin, so there's a 50-percent chance of heads and a 50-percent chance of tails. You have to pay fifty cents to play the game.

How much are you likely to win if you play this game? Not two dollars, because 50 percent of the time the coin will come up tails and you'll get nothing. Rather, the value of the game to you, the *expected benefit*, is fifty cents: the differential (two dollars) multiplied by the probability that you get it (50 percent), minus the cost—the fifty cents you pay to play the game.

Returning to Gradley vs. McBush, in order to compare the benefits and costs of voting, you have to translate the differential into an expected benefit, just as in the coin flip. That is, you have to multiply the differential by the probability that you're pivotal. The resulting expected benefit can be directly compared to the costs of voting, and you can decide whether it's worth it to go to the polls.

In a typical American presidential election, the probability that you're the pivotal voter is extremely low. Ignore the electoral college for a moment and just assume that the candidate who receives the most votes wins. About seventy million people vote in a typical presidential election. You're the pivotal voter if everyone else divides evenly—thirty-five million for McBush and thirty-five million for Gradley—and your vote breaks the tie.

What are the chances of you being the pivotal voter in the McBush vs. Gradley contest? Not zero, but very, very small. Even saying that the election is close—49.9 percent to 50.1 percent—doesn't raise the probability all that much.

Right about now, you're probably wondering, If it costs something to vote, and my vote generates benefits for me only if I'm pivotal, and the chances that I'm pivotal are extremely small, then why should I ever vote? Even if the costs of voting are small, the expected benefits are likely to be even smaller, even if you add them up across a number of races. If so, abstention would be the rational choice.

Political scientists William H. Riker and Peter C. Ordeshook label this problem the *paradox of voting*.[3] The paradox (or mystery) is this: Why does anyone vote, given that the costs of voting always (or nearly always) outweigh the benefits? The real mystery is that some people actually incur the costs of voting and go to the polls.

Why Vote? Benefits from Participation

Despite the paradox, a sizable number of Americans continue to vote. In percentage terms, turnout among registered voters in con-

[3]William H. Riker and Peter C. Ordeshook, "A Theory of the Calculus of Voting," *American Political Science Review* 62 (1968): 25–42.

temporary American elections varies from about 60 to 70 percen
presidential election years (such as 2000) to about 50 percent in ε
year elections (where there are elections for the House and Sen.
but no presidential race, such as 1998), to about 30 to 40 percent ın
odd-year elections (where no national offices are at stake, such as
1999).

Riker and Ordeshook explain the paradox by arguing that people
must receive an additional benefit from voting, one that has nothing
to do with their feelings about the candidates or the outcome of the
election. In particular, they speculate that many people receive participation benefits from the act of voting itself.

Where do these participation benefits come from? One reasonable
possibility is that people see voting as a civic duty, one that they want
to carry out.[4] Some people have a strong sense of civic duty, receive
high participation benefits from voting, and are therefore likely to
vote even when costs are high. Others have little or no sense of duty,
receive low or zero participation benefits, and will likely abstain, even
when costs are low.

If Riker and Ordeshook are right, people vote not because they
care about the outcome or because they think the election is close.
Rather, they vote because they want to, or like to, or because voting
makes them feel good. All of these interpretations are consistent with
their notion of participation benefits.

This explanation for voting has the ring of truth. Most of us are
taught from early childhood that voting is a fundamental responsibility of citizenship. And, as the saying goes, voting gives you the right
to complain about what government does and doesn't do.

It may seem touchy-feely to assume that participation benefits
exist. However, this assumption is not incompatible with saying
that people make rational choices about voting. All you need is a
wider and more accurate definition of the motivations that underlie
the decision between voting and abstaining. Why participation is
beneficial to rational actors is an interesting question, but it is not
one that you need to answer in order to understand voting as a rational choice.

Benefits, Costs, and Turnout. The decision to vote is really a decision. Abstention can be a rational choice, even when you care deeply

---

[4]This notion is similar to the discussion in Chapter Three of participation benefits as
a solution to the free-rider problem in collective action.

about the outcome of an election. Why? Because your vote is unlikely
to affect the outcome.

These findings refute the intuition that abstention is simply irrational, that it reflects a voter's indifference between the candidates or
a voter's beliefs that the race isn't close. The message here is that rational voters, voters who see significant differences between candidates who are running for office, may nevertheless abstain because
the costs of voting outweigh the benefits.

This analysis also explains the impact of changes in the benefits and
costs of voting on the likelihood of turnout. Recall that the beginning of this section stated that a citizen who sees large differences between candidates is no more likely to vote than a citizen who sees
miniscule differences, but that turnout decisions are very sensitive to
the costs of voting.

Some observers think that high turnout is a sign that citizens care
about politics, while low turnout is a sign that people are indifferent
or alienated. People who find this argument attractive see the decline
in turnout over the last generation as a sign that democracy in America is in deep trouble.

Similarly, other people argue that abstention signals that people fail
to see the importance of voting in a democracy, as a means of selecting elected officials and controlling their actions in office.

The analysis presented here suggests that both arguments are
highly suspect. Suppose you like Gradley a lot more than McBush.
However, on the day of the election, you're invited to have coffee
with someone you're attracted to. Thus, the costs of voting are, relatively speaking, high. Moreover, you don't see voting as a civic duty,
and you also know that your chances of being the pivotal voter are
very small. Accordingly, you decide against going to the polls, meet
for coffee, fall in love, and live happily ever after.

Did you abstain because you were indifferent? No. Are you alienated from politics? No. Do you know that the election matters, in the
sense that you like one candidate a lot and the other not very much?
Yes. Then why didn't you vote? Because you had something better to
do. A person who thinks turnout is important would prefer that you
combined recreation with a trip to the polling station. But your reasons for abstaining don't match either of the dire scenarios described
above.

In sum, indifference, alienation, or a lack of understanding are all
plausible explanations for why people abstain. But they are not the
only explanations. People can be highly involved in politics yet see

abstention as the choice that gives them the best payoff. Alternatively, they can see politics as a sham or an irrelevance, yet continue to vote because they see this action as an important civic duty. As a result, turnout rates don't carry much information about the health of the American political system.

Mobilization. A focus on the benefits and costs of voting should also highlight the role that mobilization efforts play in political campaigns. Mobilization involves candidates trying to "get out the vote"—ensure that supporters actually go to the polls on election day. In the main, mobilization efforts are aimed at lowering the costs of voting. These election-day calls don't involve much in the way of persuasion. The people working in these phone banks aren't going to volunteer arguments about why you should vote for their candidate—they just want to figure out a way to get you into the voting booth.[5]

For example, suppose you're a registered Republican. If so, on election day the McBush campaign is likely to call several times and remind you to vote. They'll tell you where the polling station is, ask if you need a ride or someone to walk with, offer child care if you're stuck home with the kids—in short, do anything to reduce the hassle involved with getting out to vote.

Mobilization matters because abstention is rational. From the perspective of a candidate, convincing people to like you isn't enough. Candidates must also work to increase the chances that their supporters actually vote.

Some campaigns also make antimobilization efforts. For example, during the 1990 North Carolina Senate race between Jesse Helms and Harvey Gantt, pro-Helms groups targeted neighborhoods containing a high percentage of Gantt supporters with postcards that informed citizens about criminal penalties that applied to vote fraud (i.e., voting twice, voting at the wrong address, etc.). These groups argued that they were only trying to educate the electorate. However, the type of groups targeted by these efforts suggests that the pro-Helms people were trying to lower turnout by pro-Gantt voters by scaring them into thinking that the costs of voting were higher than they thought ("Why should I vote? I might make a mistake and go to prison!")

---

[5]Another reason why campaigns focus their mobilization efforts on getting people to the polls, rather than campaigning, is that they only contact likely supporters.

Turnout and Who Wins in Politics. The analysis of turnout presented here predicts that some citizens are generally more likely to vote than others. Specifically, citizens with high participation benefits are more likely to vote than those whose participation benefits are small.

This variation in feelings about civic duty has political consequences. In general, elected officials are more likely to anticipate (or respond to) the demands of citizens who are likely voters compared to citizens who are likely to abstain.

Thus, regardless of their size, groups where participation benefits are high have a significant advantage when making demands on government: Their demands will be taken seriously because group members are likely voters. In contrast, groups in which benefits from participation are generally low often have their demands overlooked—not because the group is small or their demands outlandish, but because group members are expected to abstain.

A good example of how expectations about turnout shape the behavior of elected officials can be seen by contrasting how senior citizens get treated in the legislative process versus the treatment accorded to students. For years, members of Congress have taken special care to ensure that seniors get what they want from government. Social Security is often described as the "third rail of American politics," meaning that any attempt to change the program leads to certain (political) death for the representative who proposes it.[6]

Why such deference to senior citizens, who make up only 10 to 15 percent of the voting-age population in most districts? Because they vote. Senior citizens have one of the highest turnout rates of any group in contemporary American politics. Thus, it is no surprise that legislators are careful to keep seniors happy, as a means of staying in office.

In contrast to the deference to the concerns of senior citizens, consider how legislators treat students, who as a group have one of the highest abstention rates in contemporary American politics. Over the last twenty years, federal programs that supply student aid and student loans have either been eliminated or allowed to grow at extremely slow rates. Students lose because they do not vote. And

---

[6]You may wonder whether this statement holds in the late 1990s, especially in light of recent attempts to change the program (e.g., increase the retirement age, lower cost-of-living increases, etc.). However, it is important to note that proposed changes generally reduce benefits for *future* recipients, not current recipients. Even today, legislators are careful to accommodate demands made by seniors.

because students don't vote, their demands carry little weight in the legislative process.

Learning About the Candidates: The Problem of Cheap Talk

This section considers a second fundamental task faced by voters in an election: deciding whom to vote for. Making this choice requires voters to form judgments about how different candidates will behave if elected, then decide which one is preferable in light of their evaluations.

This section focuses on the process of appraisal and assessment that underlies voter's choices. As in the previous section, the discussion is cast in terms of a hypothetical presidential election between McBush and Gradley. You are the voter. You want to make a rational choice— you want to vote for the candidate that comes closest to your definition of a good president. What criteria or sources of information will you use to form your impressions of these two candidates?

The goal of this analysis is to explain two well-known but unusual aspects of campaigns and to show that they are compatible with the assumption of rational choice. The first anomaly is that voters ignore much of what candidates say and do. Throughout their campaign, McBush and Gradley will make many speeches, release countless issue papers and statements, and appear at a large number of town hall meetings. However, most voters ignore this information, even when it is available at no cost. The question is, why would rational voters overlook so much of what happens in a campaign, given their stated interest in voting for the right candidate?

The second campaign anomaly is that insofar as voters pay attention to anything, they focus on a candidate's appearance, personality, and private life rather than the candidate's campaign platform. Perhaps the most notable example is the political significance of ethnic food:

> No serious candidate for president can rest secure in his knowledge of the intricacies of Iowa agriculture or New Hampshire environmentalism; he must master ethnic food as well. At a minimum, he (or she) must know how to use chopsticks; how to shuck tamales; how to open a lobster; how to eat ribs; how to eat pasta standing up without getting sauce on his tie (or blouse); and when it is permissible to drink milk in a kosher deli. . . . The candidate must also how familiarity with deli food, Chinese food, soul food and barbecue, corned beef and cabbage, sauerkraut and wurst,

souvlaki and baklava, pizza, sushi, quiche, and—of course—tamales and tacos.[7]

For example, when President Ford ate an unshucked tamale during a campaign stop in Texas during the 1976 campaign, this error was thought to have reduced his standing among Mexican American voters and to have contributed to his losing Texas to Jimmy Carter in the 1976 presidential election.[8] When Ford was asked on the day after he lost the election whether he had learned anything during the campaign, he replied, "Always shuck your tamales."

Why do voters ignore issue positions and focus on a candidate's ability to eat ethnic food? It would be no surprise to find that voters tried to learn the candidate's positions only on those issues that they cared about, or ignored certain kinds of information, such as the party platform, or only gathered information that was available at low cost. But in a typical American presidential election, the average voter ignores the most obvious source of information—information about issues and positions from the candidates themselves. Moreover, they pay a lot of attention to facts that appear to have little connection to politics or to governing.

This section shows that both of these apparent anomalies are, in fact, the result of rational calculation. Forming judgments based on what candidates say assumes that they are telling the truth. Suppose McBush promises to cut taxes, raise government spending, and cure the common cold. Can these promises be taken seriously?

The answer depends on three factors: the nature of the promise or position, the candidate's motives, and how easy it is for the candidate to misrepresent the truth. In campaigns where candidates want to impress voters in order to win their election and where truthfulness is hard to verify, it makes sense that the electorate ignores much of what candidates say.

This analysis also explains why voters pay so much attention to a candidate's appearance and personal life. Factors such as a candidate's race or gender are informative because policy preferences vary across these groups in society and because appearance is something that candidates cannot manipulate. A candidate's marital status, military

---

[7]Samuel L. Popkin, *The Reasoning Voter* (Chicago: University of Chicago Press, 1991), p. 2.

[8]Tamales consist of a meat or corn-based filling with a cornhusk covering. The husks are used as a wrapping, taste awful, and are not supposed to be eaten.

service, or similar actions can be interpreted in the same way. In other words, looking outside politics to form judgments about candidates is an eminently rational choice.

Making Sense of a Candidate's Signals

Suppose you face the choice between McBush and Gradley. Your criteria are simple: You want to elect a president who is opposed to raising taxes, no matter what. That's the only issue you care about. Defense spending, welfare policy, foreign relations, preservation of the Spotted Owl—none of that matters. Your only concern is to find a candidate who won't raise your taxes.

Each candidate knows his true intentions regarding tax increases. Your task is to determine these intentions, based on the information that becomes available to you during the campaign, in order to vote for the candidate whose tax policies are closest to your ideal.

In particular, suppose that during their acceptance speeches at their party's conventions, the candidates each made the following statements:[9]

McBush: The Congress will push me to raise taxes and I'll say no, and they'll push, and I'll say no, and they'll push again, and I'll say to them, "Read my lips, no new taxes."

Gradley: Let's tell the truth. Mr. McBush will raise taxes and so will I. He won't tell you. I just did.

Which of these candidates should you believe? McBush, who said what you and most voters want to hear? Gradley, whose position appears to be the opposite of your own? Or should you ignore both of these statements? You happened to have been watching TV at the time of the speeches, so you received this information at no cost. The question is, what should you do with it?

Truth telling in elections is only one example of a generic situation that occurs both inside and outside politics. Think about buying a used car. You want cheap, reliable transportation, so you go to Shady Al's Used Car Emporium.[10] Because Al's sales staff is working on

[9]These quotes are based on George Bush's speech to the 1988 Republican Convention and Walter Mondale's speech at the 1984 Democratic Convention.
[10]I hereby apologize in advance to anyone who has a relative named Al who sells or has sold used cars.

commission, they have a considerable incentive to say good things about the cars on their lot. Their statements are hard to prove or disprove. If, for example, you are told that a car you're interested in was only driven to and from Sunday school, should you believe this statement or disregard it?

Candidates for office aren't used-car salespeople—or at least not usually. Even so, the problem faced by voters when forming judgments based on what candidates say is much the same as the one faced by anyone walking onto a used-car lot. And the rules for how to interpret their statements are exactly the same as the ones you should use to interpret claims made by Shady Al or one of his minions.

In the abstract, the situation is as follows: One person, a sender, makes a statement. After the sender's move, a second person, the receiver, interprets this statement. Here, the two statements you (the receiver) need to assess are McBush's and Gradley's promises regarding tax increases.

In the case of McBush and Gradley, voters, having heard each candidate's statement, must consider whether it reveals anything about their true intentions. If, for example, McBush promises not to raise taxes, will he really follow through? Or is McBush planning to raise taxes as soon as he is elected? And what about Gradley's promise to raise taxes? Is that promise more credible—and if so, why?

The answer can be described in terms of three questions:

- The sender's motives—does she have reason to misrepresent the truth?
- The nature of the statement—is it what the receiver wants to hear?
- The ability to misrepresent—is it costly for the sender to misrepresent the truth?

Each of these questions will be discussed separately.

The Sender's Motives. When interpreting signals, your first task is to determine the motives of the sender. In particular, does the sender want you to learn the truth about the factors she is describing?

Think about buying a used car at Shady Al's. You can pick from two salespersons: George Washington, the father of our country and protector of all Americans, who cannot tell a lie; and John Lovitz, the Pathological Liar from *Saturday Night Live*. Which salesperson is more likely to say things that you can believe? Washington would like to sell you a car, but he also wants you to be happy with your purchase. Lovitz, on the other hand, wants to sell cars and thereby maximize his income from commissions.

Obviously, you would be more likely to believe Washington. His interests are compatible with your own: You want to buy a good car, and he wants you to be happy with the car you buy. So if he tells you that a car is in good shape and well worth buying, you can take this statement seriously. For if the car had significant defects, Washington would tell you to avoid it, since his primary goal is to make sure you're satisfied with your purchase.

In contrast, suppose that Lovitz made the same statements. Now you should be much more suspicious. After all, Lovitz's motivation is to sell you a car—he doesn't care about your satisfaction after the sale. Even if he knew that the car was in bad shape, he would misrepresent the truth, as a way of convincing you to buy it.

How does the contrast between Washington and Lovitz help you to interpret the promises of McBush and Gradley? It confirms that it's rational for you to be suspicious. Each of these candidates wants to win the election and, therefore, has a strong incentive to say or do whatever is necessary to win voter's support.

The point is not that McBush and Gradley always lie or that they misrepresent their positions whenever it's necessary to win support. Rather, in a world where candidates for office want to win, their statements cannot be taken at face value. Most politicians will claim that they are men or women of principle, who "tell it like it is," even if it costs them an election. But do they mean it? They may be revealing their intentions accurately, or they may be saying things that are designed to attract support. If you can't be sure, then the truth of everything else they say is open to question.

The Nature of the Statement. The second rule is that you should be suspicious of signals that are consistent with impressions or judgments that a sender wants you to form. Conversely, signals that lead to judgments that are harmful to the sender are much more likely to be truthful.

Again consider buying a used car at Shady Al's. You're standing in front of a car with a salesperson named Jane Average (Washington and Lovitz are both in a meeting). To keep the example simple, assume that there are no other possible cars on the lot—if you pass up this one, you're going to look elsewhere. Also, you're not sure about

Average's motives—you don't know whether she's a Washington or a Lovitz.

Consider how you'd react when Average says one of two things:

- "This car is a creampuff, driven only to church on Sundays by a sweet little old lady, except on the first Monday of every month, when she took it to the Good News Garage for servicing."[11]
- "This car was driven three times on the Trans-Africa rally by a driver who was later banned for excessive abuse of automotive machinery, and has never had its oil changed."

The first statement should raise some suspicions. You're not sure about Average's motives, but it's possible that she's like Lovitz and only wants to sell you a car at the highest possible price. Put another way, she may be telling you the truth, but it's just as likely that she is misrepresenting the car's true condition in order to push you into buying it.

Now consider the second statement. By saying bad things about the vehicle, Jane Average is working against the goal of selling you a car—if you take the statement seriously, you will look elsewhere, and Average will lose a commission. Thus, this statement has a better chance of being true, as there's no chance that Average is misrepresenting the car's true condition.

This discussion suggests a simple rule about how to interpret a candidate's statements: Be suspicious of statements that are consistent with beliefs and preferences that are widely held in the electorate; take seriously statements that contradict these beliefs and preferences.

For example, candidate McBush promises not to raise taxes. Most voters oppose tax increases. Thus, McBush is saying what voters want to hear. He may be telling the truth, but it's very possible that his promise is designed to impress voters and win their support. Put another way, a rational actor would listen to McBush and conclude, "McBush says he wants to keep taxes low, but everyone knows that he wants to win the election, and therefore has reason to say things that voters like. Unless I have some other reason for thinking he's telling the truth, I'm going to disregard his statement."

[11]The Good News Garage is located in Cambridge, Mass. and is owned by the Car Guys, a.k.a. Click and Clack, hosts of *Car Talk* on National Public Radio.

In contrast, Gradley promises to raise taxes. Upon hearing it, a rational actor would say, "Since the promise is the opposite of what voters want, it must be the truth, for why would Gradley make this promise, unless he really favored a tax increase?" Gradley's commitment is a political loser—most voters want lower taxes, not higher. Thus, the promise can't be aimed at winning the election. If winning was all Gradley cared about, he would have kept quiet or made a promise like McBush's. Therefore, there's a very good chance that Gradley's promise reflects the candidate's true intentions and should be taken seriously.

The Ability to Misrepresent. One of the most important factors that shape the rational response to a signal is whether it is easy (costless) for a sender to misrepresent the truth. The rule is simple: When it's easy for a sender to lie, disregard what she says, unless there's some other reason to take the signal seriously, such as the nature of what's being said or the sender's motives. Conversely, when it's hard, impossible, or very costly for the sender to lie, you should listen carefully to the signal and take actions based on what you hear.

Take yourself back to Shady Al's. You find a car you like. Salesperson Jane Average tells you that the car's a creampuff, and invites you to kick the tires and take it for a spin. Now comes decision time. Should you accept Jane Average's statements or disregard them?

You don't know enough about Jane Average's motives to determine whether she will lie if necessary to close a sale. And Jane Average has made positive statements about the car, so you can't use the nature of the promise rule to decide whether she's telling the truth.

One final possibility is to consider whether it's costly for Jane Average to misrepresent the car's true condition. Consider two scenarios:

• Jane Average is a salesperson you've met today for the first time.
• Jane Average is your second cousin.

In the first scenario, there's no reason to take Average's claims seriously—besides all of the other factors discussed up to now, misrepresenting the truth is costless to Average. Once you buy the car, you'll drive away and never see her again. Economists refer to statements made under these conditions as "cheap talk." When talk is cheap, you shouldn't place much weight on what you hear.

The second scenario describes a situation where misrepresenting the truth could be costly. Suppose you have a close extended family: Every Sunday you all gather at Grandma Average's house for dinner, touch football, and group folk sings. These ties create a situation where misrepresenting the car's true condition is costly for Average.

Imagine what happens if Cousin Jane tells you that the car's a creampuff when it's actually a wreck. You may miss Sunday dinner because of a breakdown. When you get there, you'll spoil the gathering with your complaints, and your grandmother will yell at Jane for taking advantage of a family member.

If Jane Average is a rational actor (and even car salespeople are), she will anticipate the bad consequences (to her) of selling you a lemon. From her perspective, misrepresenting the truth about a bad car is costly—you'll be angry, your grandmother will be angry, and her Sunday dinner will forever be spoiled. The existence of these costs changes her calculations and makes revelation of the car's true condition her best strategy, regardless of whether the information causes you to buy the car or look elsewhere.

Knowing the constraints that Average faces, the rational response is to accept her statements about the car, regardless of whether they are positive or negative. The reason is not the existence of family ties. Rather, it is the potential penalty associated with being caught lying that makes your cousin's claims mean something.

What do these scenarios say about the campaign between McBush and Gradley? Most of the things that candidates say and do during a campaign are good examples of cheap talk—it doesn't cost a candidate anything to promise something to the voters. Candidates make all sorts of promises but are usually careful to add exceptions and wiggle room. That is, they don't promise to keep taxes low, they promise to *fight* to keep taxes low or to work with Congress to prevent tax increases. Adding these "weasel words" helps a politician argue that she kept to her word, even as she caves completely. However, it transforms concrete promises into cheap talk.

When is campaign talk not cheap? When a candidate makes a pledge like McBush's: ". . . Read my lips: no new taxes." This promise is simple and easy to understand. It will attract support from the many voters who favor lower taxes. Moreover, voters can tell if McBush keeps his word: All they have to do is see if he supports any tax increases while in office.

McBush has to weigh his words carefully. If he promises "no new taxes" then reneges after a few years, he will lose support from people who liked the no-taxes promise, as well as support from people who won't vote for a candidate who reneged on a promise. Put another way, McBush faces a situation where misrepresenting the truth—pledging no new taxes when his intentions differ—is costly.

If you're a rational actor, and you know that McBush will lose many votes if he reneges on his pledge, how should you respond? You should take the promise seriously. Why? Because no candidate who had any intention of raising taxes while in office would ever make such a pledge.[12] In other words, McBush can't be making this pledge to attract support. So, his pledge must reflect his true intentions and should be taken seriously.

Candidate Signals: A Summary. This discussion of how rational actors respond to signals shows that the contest between McBush and Gradley is a very special case: Both of the candidates' promises about taxes can be taken seriously.

Gradley's promise to raise taxes will cost him votes because it is contrary to what most voters want. Thus, the promise is likely to reflect his true intentions.

McBush promises to keep taxes where they are, which at first glance is a promise you should ignore. But it's a simple, clear promise, which makes it easy to hold McBush accountable if he reneges. Therefore, since McBush faces significant costs if he misrepresents his true intentions (says he won't raise taxes and later does), the promise should be believed.

Why are these special cases? Because most of the time, politicians steer clear of promises that hurt their chances of getting reelected (such as Gradley's) as well as promises that they can be held accountable for (such as McBush's). The first kind of promise hurts your chances of getting elected now, while the second can damage your chances later.

To put it another way, in most campaigns, voters are well aware that candidates want to win the election, and they are well aware that this goal motivates candidates to promise whatever constituents want

---

[12]If you know some history, you're probably thinking, "But George Bush really made this pledge in 1988, and reneged on it in 1991. Either Bush was irrational for making the pledge knowing that he might renege, or voters were irrational because they believed him in the first place." However, the fact that people are rational doesn't mean they don't make mistakes. In this case, the most likely explanation is that Bush believed that, after the Gulf War, his popularity was so high that reneging on the no-tax promise would not cost him significant support.

in order to win their support. Under these conditions, it is rational for constituents to ignore most of what candidates tell them during the campaign. The problem is not that voters aren't interested in choosing the right candidate or that it's too much trouble to think through the implications of what candidates say. Rather, the problem is that candidates cannot be relied on to tell the truth.

Does this finding imply that rational voters ignore everything candidates say? As the example of McBush and Gradley indicates, the answer is No. Voters will pay attention when a candidate's promise is politically costly, sufficiently concise that the candidate can be held accountable for reneging, or made by a candidate with a reputation for truth telling. Under these conditions, a rational candidate would tell the truth, so rational constituents are primed to listen carefully.

While this strategy is completely rational, it may cause voters to overlook valuable information. Suppose, for example, that Gradley changed his promise, saying that he would raise taxes only to prevent a large rise in the deficit. That promise may accurately reflect Gradley's intentions. However, because the promise is vague (when are tax increases the only option? How large is a "large rise" in the deficit?), voters are likely to see it as cheap talk and ignore it, even though it's a completely true statement. However, the fact that voters disregard Gradley's new promise doesn't mean they are behaving irrationally. Rather, they are responding optimally to the situation as they see it. Lacking the ability to hook Gradley up to a polygraph, the vagueness of the promise, coupled with the knowledge that Gradley wants to attract support to win the election, makes ignoring the promise a rational choice.

Beyond Promises: Actions and Appearance

As you have seen, it is often a rational strategy for voters to ignore what candidates say during the course of a campaign. Why? Because voters can't be sure whether candidates are telling the truth or lying. This explanation answers only part of the puzzle of how voters appraise candidates. The other task is to explain why voters pay so much attention to a candidate's race, gender, ethnicity, past actions, and actions that appear to have no connection to politics.

Rational voters consider these factors for the same reason they sometimes listen to what candidates say: to make judgments about how candidates will behave if elected. The advantage of considering appearance or past actions rather than statements is that a candidate cannot manipulate these factors in order to shape the inferences that voters draw.

For example, return to the McBush and Gradley example. You want to determine where these candidates stand on raising taxes. One morning during a conversation with your neighbor, you learn that McBush was an undergraduate at a well-known ivy-covered university in New Haven, Connecticut. In his senior year, he served as president of the student body and implemented several large increases in the mandatory activity fee.

What does that information tell you about McBush? One plausible inference you might make is that McBush isn't fundamentally opposed to raising taxes—after all, he increased student activity fees. Your inference may be wrong: McBush may have changed his mind about the wisdom of tax increases or may see taxes as fundamentally different from activity fees. Even so, it seems reasonable that hearing about McBush's career in college politics might cause you to discount his no-tax pledge.

Similarly, what if your neighbor also tells you that in addition to attending that well-known ivy-covered university in New Haven, McBush was born into a well-to-do Texas family and did his high school years at a ritzy prep school in New England.

What do you learn from McBush's family and educational background? That he's a member of the upper class and, as such, might define a tax increase in terms of how it affects people he knows. In other words, changes in tax laws that primarily effect people of lesser means, such as increased taxes on alcohol or cigarettes or increased withholding for Social Security, might not look like a tax increase to McBush, although they will increase the government's receipts.

Factors such as a candidate's past actions or his appearance play a critical role in American elections. Why? First, it's easy to use these factors to form impressions. It is as though a voter learns something about a candidate and thinks, "The candidate has this characteristic, people holding this characteristic tend to be of a particular type (or hold certain policy preferences), so I will conclude there is a good chance the candidate is of that type."

Think about yourself. If I told you that a candidate was female, or African American, or a devout Mormon, or a graduate of Yale, each piece of information would call to mind an image of what this person is like and what kinds of policies she might prefer. Most people, for example, would assume that an African American candidate favors liberal social-welfare policies and cuts in defense spending. This judgment will not always be correct (there are several conservative African American members of Congress whose preferences differ from this stereotype), but is likely to be true on average.

The second advantage of inferences based on a candidate's appearance or past actions is that these factors are difficult if not impossible to manipulate. Statements, in contrast, often amount to cheap talk—a candidate can just as easily make one promise as another. This flexibility does not exist for appearance and past actions. An African American candidate cannot change her skin color in order to appeal to voters who favor increases in defense spending. McBush cannot erase his record as student body president or alter the fact that he was born holding a silver spoon. Therefore, a voter can use these factors to make judgments about a candidate's intentions without worrying that he is being deliberately misled.

You may think that it's absurd for a voter to link a candidate's past actions with their present intentions and that it's even worse to base judgments on a candidate's appearance or actions outside politics. Before you do, consider one of the extreme examples: Gerald Ford's tussle with the unshucked tamale.[13]

Why would Mexican Americans focus on Ford's knowledge of their cuisine? Sam Popkin gives the answer: "Would a Mexican American voter who saw President Ford bite into an unshucked tamale be wrong to conclude that the President had little experience with Mexican-American culture, little feel for it?"[14] Tamale-eating seems far away from politics, but, in fact, knowledge of a group's culture is a first step to knowing what they want from government. By holding Ford accountable for his lack of knowledge of tamales, Mexican American voters were not being myopic or vindictive—rather, they were being reasonably astute.

Most candidates accommodate the electorate's desire for personal information. Indeed, a sizable fraction of what happens during a campaign consists of highlighting bits and pieces of a candidate's past that are expected to generate support among the voters.

Consider how Bill Clinton was described during 1992 as a "man from Hope," advertising the fact that he grew up in the very small town of Hope, Arkansas. This choice is not random. It reflects the

---

[13]This story concerns an action taken during a campaign, but it can be interpreted the same way as an action taken in the past.
[14]Popkin, 1991, p. 3.

widespread American belief that virtue, honor, and other good qualities are more likely to be found in small towns than in big cities.

Clinton's opponent, George Bush, described himself as a "man with a mission," reflecting his service as a naval aviator in World War II. Again, the Bush campaign was trying to highlight a choice—military service—which voters might see as an indication of Bush's overall attractiveness as a candidate.

In sum, it makes sense for rational voters to use a candidate's appearance and past actions in order to make judgments about how the candidate is likely to behave in office. This information is easy to use. Moreover, these factors are difficult or impossible for candidates to manipulate.

The search for past actions as a source of information about candidates explains why politics is sometimes so personal—why nothing in a candidate's history or personal life seems to be beyond scrutiny. In trying to learn everything they can about a candidate, even things well outside politics, voters are not being nosy or gossips. Rather, they are trying to find a source of information that is not contaminated by political considerations.

Summary

This chapter has considered how voters make two fundamental decisions: whether they should vote and how they should gather information about the candidates. The analysis reveals many surprises about what it means to cast a rational vote. Rational citizens can abstain rather than vote. And rational voters may base their decisions on seemingly irrelevant information such as a candidate's race, gender, and past actions, rather than on detailed information about the candidate's platforms.

This discussion of rationality in voting also helps to make sense of what happens during real-world campaigns. Why, for example, do citizens who say they have strong feelings about the candidates nevertheless decide against voting? Why do voters often focus on a candidate's personal life? And why do voters often say that they want to learn about candidates' issue positions yet ignore most of the information delivered to them during the campaign?

This chapter has shown that all of these apparent anomalies in voter behavior have simple explanations, explanations that are consistent with voters being rational actors.

You may be disturbed that rational people can decide to abstain or to vote based on seemingly trivial factors such as a candidate's knowledge of ethnic cuisine. However, saying that a person is rational doesn't imply that she takes socially desirable actions, spends a lot of time deciding what to do, or acts based on all available information. What rationality means is that people make the best choices they can, given what they want, the options open to them, and the constraints on their behavior. Based on that standard, voters in American elections are thoroughly rational actors.

~5~

Winning and Holding Elective Office

T his chapter focuses on the essence of democracy: how citizens' preferences influence what politicians say and do, both at election time and in between elections.

The first section focuses on how rational candidates choose campaign platforms. The aim is to show how the goal of winning office forces candidates to consider and accommodate voters' preferences, choosing platforms that reflect the preferences of voters in the middle of their district's ideological spectrum.

The analysis also explains a well-known anomaly, that candidates running for the same office often take similar if not the same positions on most issues. Intuitively, elections should involve a choice between alternate visions of what government should do. Yet in many campaigns, such as the 2000 Democratic and Republican races for the presidential nomination, after you subtract oratory, humor, and the occasional dumb mistake, candidates often wind up sounding alike.

Consider one reporter's analysis of a debate in fall 1999 between the Democratic candidates, Al Gore and Bill Bradley:[1]

[1]Richard L. Berke, "Gore and Bradley Agree More Than Disagree at Forum," *New York Times,* October 28, 1999. http://www.nytimes.com/library/politics/camp/102899wh-dem-debate.html

. . . on a wide array of issues, the two candidates for the Democratic Presidential nomination agreed more than they disagreed as they appealed to
liberal primary voters for stepped-up financing on mental health, special
education and environmental measures and for more stringent laws protecting homosexuals.

The title of an article about a debate involving Republican candidates
suggests a similar level of agreement: "5 G.O.P. Candidates Gather
for Talk but Little Sparring."[2] Thus the question: Why do candidates
wind up choosing similar platforms?

The second part of the chapter describes how elected officials respond to voters' demands in between elections. In particular, this
section explains why constituents sometimes trust their legislator's
judgment, even when her actions look suspicious. While trust allows
legislators to use their judgment when voting, it also enables them to
ignore their constituents' demands without fear of retribution in the
next election. Thus the question: Why would rational constituents
decide to trust their representative?

The answer is that trust makes sense when constituents are poorly
informed about the details of policy proposals and believe that their
representative's interests are compatible with their own. To show you
that these criteria are not some academic's fantasy about how constituents should act, the analysis focuses on a real-world example, a
pay raise for members of Congress that was enacted in 1989.

At first glance, you might think that pay-raise proposals are the last
place to look for trust, on grounds that most voters strongly oppose
these measures. For example, when describing their constituents'
reaction to an earlier raise proposal, House members used words
like "vociferous," "visceral," "violent," "virulent," "vehement," and
"vituperative" to describe the reaction. Constituents had the raise
"shoved up their nose"; they were "stirred up," "inflamed," and
"whipped into a frenzy"; they "sent letters with short, angry sentences and language I can't repeat."[3]

Yet in the case of the pay raise, enacted in the Ethics Act of 1989,
while many voters initially opposed the proposal, a substantial
number decided to allow their representative to vote as he thought

[2]Richard L. Berke with Melinda A. Henneberger, *New York Times*, October 29,
1999. http://www.nytimes.com/library/politics/camp/102999wh-gop-debate.html
[3]William T. Bianco, *Trust: Representatives and Constituents* (Ann Arbor: University
of Michigan Press, 1994), p. 4.

best. Moreover, these decisions about trust were consistent with the rational-choice explanation developed here.

Voters, Candidates, and Election Outcomes

From a voter's perspective, elections are about deciding which candidate will do a better job. This chapter moves one step back and considers how candidates choose their platforms—a series of promises about how they will behave if elected. The central question is, What does a winning platform look like? Put another way, if candidates cared only about getting elected, what kind of platform would they choose?

Of course, not all candidates *only* care about winning. Virtually all candidates want to win their elections. Some have no other goals. But most candidates hold policy goals as well—they don't just want to win, they also want to change what government is doing, such as increasing funding for the military, enacting universal health insurance, or some similar goals.

If relatively few candidates are mere election seekers, why use this assumption in the analysis of campaign platforms? Because once you know how election seekers behave (what kinds of platform they choose to maximize their chances of winning), you also know how the election goal influences the behavior of candidates who care about enacting good policies as well as getting elected.

In other words, a pure election seeker finds a platform by asking, "Which platform maximizes my chances of winning?" A more typical candidate, one who wants to be elected but who also holds some policy goals, is likely to choose a different platform. Why? Because this candidate cares about enacting good policies and may be unwilling to behave as the election-maximizing platform requires. The candidate may prefer a ban on abortion, for example, despite the fact that a prochoice position would attract more votes.

However, even when a candidate cares about policy and getting elected, her platform is likely to contain many of the same positions and promises included in the platform that a pure election seeker would run on. Why? Because if the candidate takes positions that are politically unpopular, she risks losing the election. Thus, by determining what kind of platform maximizes a candidate's chances of winning, you can gain insight into the platforms chosen by both kinds of candidates, both the pure election seeker and the candidate who holds other goals as well.

In concrete terms, suppose that voters can be arranged in a line, relatively liberal on one end, moderate in the middle, relatively conservative on the other end. Where on this spectrum will candidates try to locate themselves? For the purposes of winning an election, is a relatively extreme platform best? Or will candidates move to the middle of their district's spectrum and, if so, by how much?

Focusing on winning platforms also explains *Wallace's Law*, an observation made by George Wallace, governor of Alabama and presidential candidate in the 1968, 1972, and 1976 elections. During the 1968 campaign, when Wallace was running as an independent candidate for president, he argued that the platforms of the two major-party candidates, Richard Nixon and Hubert Humphrey, were essentially identical. As Wallace often said, "There's not a dime's worth of difference between those two candidates."

Of course, Wallace's Law is not completely right. Even in the 2000 presidential primaries, while there appears to have been considerable agreement among Democratic candidates and among Republicans, it would be too strong to say that candidates within each party held exactly the same positions or that there were no differences between the two groups of candidates. Even so, it is striking that the candidates don't try very hard to distinguish themselves from each other, preferring instead to campaign on similar platforms.

Why do rational candidates choose to advocate the same things? Put another way, why do voters reward candidates for sounding the same and punish candidates who offer them a choice? You will see that the answer lies in the fact that candidates want to win elections. This motivation drives them toward the middle of the electorate, toward platforms that replicate the policy preferences and concerns held by relatively moderate voters. Candidates may not want to sound the same, but the logic of winning elections leads them to do so.

A Spatial Model of Elections

This section's analysis of campaign platforms uses a *spatial model*.[4] A simple spatial model, such as the one in Figure 5.1, describes voters' policy preferences and candidates' platforms as points on a line. Each

---

[4]See Anthony Downs, *The Spatial Theory of Voting* (New York: Harper and Row, 1957).

FIGURE 5.1
A Simple Spatial Model

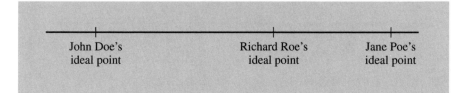

voter has an *ideal point,* a point on the line that summarizes or describes what the voter's most-preferred set of government policies
looks like.

What does the line represent? One way to think of it is in terms of
the difference between liberals and conservatives. Liberal voters have
ideal points that are on the left-hand side of the line, and conservative voters have ideal points on the right-hand side. More moderate
voters are in the middle.

People with ideal points on the left-hand side of the line, such as
John Doe in Figure 5.1, are liberals—they want an activist government that regulates the economy and commerce, protects civil liber-
ties, provides a wide range of social-welfare benefits, and doesn't
restrict private behavior.

A voter whose ideal point falls in the middle of the line, such as
Richard Roe in Figure 5.1, is a moderate and favors some economic
regulation but not too much, social-welfare programs that address
problems but don't go overboard, and moderate protection of civil
rights, and private behavior.

Finally, conservative voters have ideal points at the right-hand side
of Figure 5.1. An example is Jane Poe. The location of Poe's ideal
point implies that she supports policies such as little to no regulation
of the economy, minimal social-welfare spending, few explicit protec-
tions of civil rights, and restrictions on certain behaviors.

You might ask, aren't some people liberal on certain issues and
conservative on others? For example, a Libertarian voter might favor
no regulation of the economy but also no restrictions on individual
behavior. Can a spatial model describe these preferences? The answer
is yes. More complicated spatial models describe voter preferences in
terms of multiple dimensions. However, for the purposes of this
chapter, a single dimension is both sufficiently complicated and sufficiently interesting.

FIGURE 5.2
Roe's Preference and the Candidates' Platforms

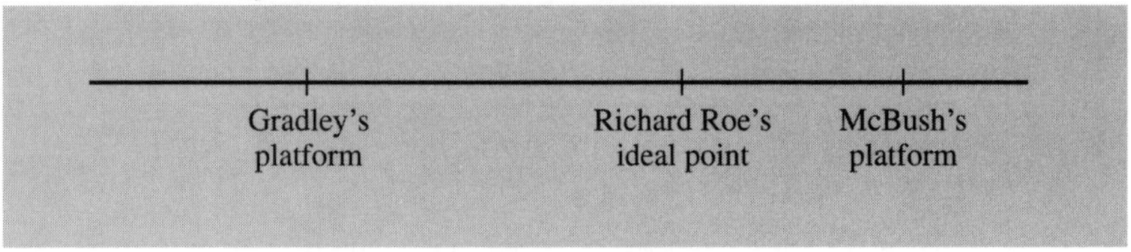

Gradley's   Richard Roe's   McBush's
platform   ideal point   platform

Why Spatial Models? Specifying voters' preferences and candidates' platforms in terms of points on a line has two advantages right off. First, it's easy to specify what it means for an individual to vote for the candidate she likes the most. In a spatial model, the right candidate for a specific voter is the one whose platform is closest to the voter's own ideal point. Figure 5.2 provides an illustration.

In the figure Richard Roe faces a choice between the two hypothetical candidates from Chapter Four: McBush and Gradley. The figure shows Roe's ideal point, along with points representing the campaign platforms of each candidate. Which candidate does Roe like best? McBush, because McBush's platform is closest to Roe's ideal point. Given a choice between these two candidates, Roe would be expected to vote for McBush.

The second advantage of describing voters' preferences and candidates' platforms in spatial terms is that it provides an easy way to summarize the preferences of large numbers of voters, such as everyone in a district, state, or nation.

Suppose that McBush and Gradley are competing for the presidency under a somewhat different set of rules than the ones described in Chapter Two. Instead of using the electoral college, everyone casts one vote, and the candidate who receives the most votes wins.

Given this assumption, the critical factor for McBush and Gradley is the distribution of voters' ideal points—how all the voters in America are arranged on the line or dimension shown in the two preceding figures. Figure 5.3 shows two possibilities.

Take a look at the top plot in Figure 5.3. The horizontal axis shows the range of possible ideal points for voters, with liberals on the left and conservatives on the right. The curve shows the number of people who hold a particular ideal point (this number is given in approximate terms by the scale on the left-hand side of the page).

FIGURE 5.3
The Median Voter and Candidates' Platforms

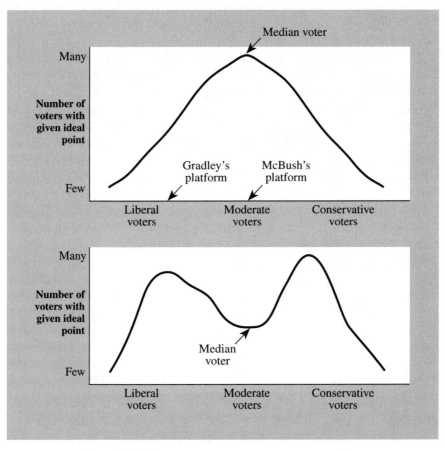

In real-world terms, the top plot describes a situation where most voters hold moderate or middle-of-the-road policy preferences. Note that the line peaks in the middle of the figure, where moderate ideal points are located, and tails off toward each extreme. Thus, most voters in this example favor candidates with moderate platforms, although there are some voters with extremely conservative or liberal ideal points, who would much prefer an extreme candidate.

The final thing to identify in Figure 5.3 is the location of the *median voter*—the voter whose ideal point is in the middle of the distribution, or the fiftieth percentile. This is the point where exactly half the voter ideal points fall to the left and half fall to the right. The fig-

doesn't contain enough information for you to find the median
r's ideal point by yourself. Having constructed the figure, I know
where it is located: right under the peak or high point in the graph.
In other words, the median voter in this example is a voter holding
moderate policy preferences.[5]

The bottom plot in Figure 5.3 shows a very different distribution
of ideal points, one where the electorate is much more diverse—
and extreme. Rather than having most ideal points bunched in the
middle, voters here are pulled to two extremes—one group on
the liberal end, the other on the conservative end. In substantive
terms, this example is one where voters tend to disagree on what a
good platform looks like. Many voters want a candidate who will advance a liberal policy agenda, but many others want a conservative
candidate.

The other thing to notice about the bottom plot is that the median
voter is located in the middle of the distribution, at the exact point
where the distribution of ideal points stops going down and begins
to rise again. In other words, even though the distribution of voters
is very different in these two plots, their median voter has the same
moderate ideal point and policy preferences. It is important to note
that, unlike the first case, the median voter in the second case does
not represent the majority of voters.

Predictions about Candidates' Platforms and Election Outcomes

This section uses the principles of spatial modeling to describe what
winning platforms look like for each of the electorates shown in Figure 5.3. Put another way, if McBush and Gradley only cared about
winning their election, which platform would they choose—where
would each candidate locate his platform on the line that runs from
liberal to moderate to conservative?

Consider the top plot in Figure 5.3, an electorate where there are
many moderate voters and a few at the liberal and conservative extremes. Where is each candidate's winning platform? If both candidates want to win the election, then they will select the same
platform, the one that matches the preferences held by the median

---

[5]It's not inevitable that the median voter be a moderate. For example, in a district
dominated by conservative voters, the median voter might be a strong conservative,
with extreme conservatives on one side and somewhat less conservative voters on the
other.

voter in the electorate. If for some reason a candidate cannot locate his platform at the median, he will try to get as close as possible.

Why is the median a winning platform? If a candidate is a rational actor who wants to win and who expects her opponent to be rational, this location maximizes the candidate's share of the vote and thus maximizes her chances of winning the election.

To see this logic, suppose that McBush located his platform at the median, while Gradley selected a platform that was located at some distance towards the left-hand side of the distribution. This scenario is shown in Figure 5.3.

Given these placements, McBush would win the election for sure. Why? Remember that people vote for the platform that's closest to their ideal point. If so, people with ideal points to the right of the dotted line in Figure 5.3 will vote for McBush, while people with ideal points on the left side of the line will vote for Gradley. Clearly, McBush will receive more votes and win the election.

The only way for Gradley to increase his share of the vote is to move his platform closer to the median voter's ideal point. As Gradley moves in to the median, he gains votes and McBush loses votes, as more voters find that Gradley's new platform is closer to their ideal point than the median platform selected by McBush. Even so, as long as Gradley's platform is not at the median and McBush's is, McBush will attract more votes and win the election.

Where does this process end? Assuming both candidates only care about winning, the expectation is that they will run on identical platforms that match the ideal point of the median voter. Thus, the prediction of the spatial model is that an election-seeking candidate will move to the median, even if the result is that he runs on the same platform as the one chosen by his opponent.

This prediction does not depend on having a neat, single-peaked distribution of voters' ideal points as in the top plot of Figure 5.3. Consider the bottom plot in Figure 5.3, an electorate where there are two distinct peaks in the distribution of voters. One sensible intuition is that the candidates maximize their chances of winning by locating their platforms under one of the peaks in the distribution. That is, Gradley would pick a platform that matched the ideal point of the left-hand peak, while McBush would select a platform that corresponded to the right-hand peak.

This intuition is wrong. Even in the case of the second electorate, both candidates do best by locating their platforms at the median. In other words, as long as the two plots in Figure 5.3 have the same me-

dian, the distribution of voters in those electorates (how many liberals, how many moderates, and how many conservatives) doesn't matter.

The similarity in predictions for the two electorates is no accident.
It is an example of one of the first and most influential results derived
from spatial modeling, the *median voter theorem*. This theorem, developed fifty years ago by Duncan Black,[6] states that

- if voters' policy preferences and candidates' platforms can be expressed as points on a line,
- and if candidates are able to choose whatever platform they want
  to,
- and if voters choose the candidate whose platform is closest to
  their ideal point, and flip a coin if platforms are equally distant,
- and if candidates only care about winning the election,

then both candidates' platforms will be identical to the median
voter's ideal point. The distribution of voter preferences on the policy dimension doesn't matter. You can move voters' ideal points
around in Figure 5.3 as much as you want and, as long as you don't
change the location of the median voter, the candidates' platform
choices stay the same. If, however, you change the location of the
median voter, then the predictions about platforms will change as
well—candidates will shift to place themselves on top of the new median.

Will Candidates Always Move to the Median?

The spatial model supplies clear advice to election-minded candidates: move to the median. By matching the median voter's ideal
point, candidates maximize their chances of winning the general election.

It is important to understand that candidates for Congress and
other offices might not fully implement this advice. They may see the
electoral value of moving their platform close to the median voter's
ideal point, but nevertheless decide to run on a nonmedian platform.
This choice doesn't mean they are irrational or dumb, it just means
that their decision is influenced by other factors. This section de-

[6]Duncan Black and R. A. Newing, *Committee Decisions with Complementary Valua-
tion* (London: William Hodge and Company, 1951).

scribes three factors that might keep candidates off the median: cɪ ibility, primary elections, and personal policy goals.

Limits on Credible Platforms. One obvious limitation on a candidate's selection of a platform is the electorate's willingness to take the choice seriously. As noted in Chapter Four, rational voters disregard many of the promises candidates make. In terms of platform choices, this skepticism implies that candidates may be unable to campaign on median platforms even if they want to.

Why are a candidate's platform choices limited? Suppose candidate Gradley, a Democrat, only cares about winning the general election and, having read Black's median-voter theorem, tries to campaign on a platform than matches the ideal point of the median voter. The problem is, voters have other information available to them, information that may lead them to discount Gradley's promises.

For one thing, voters know that Gradley is a Democrat and that Democrats tend to be liberal on most issues. So if Gradley tries to make moderate promises, a voter might respond, "Well, that's very interesting, but you're a Democrat, and Democrats tend to be liberal, so I'm unwilling to take your median platform at face value. Instead, I'll assume that your true platform is somewhere to the left of the median voter."

In addition, most candidates for president have held other offices and have a record of public statements, votes, and other indications of their beliefs about good public policy. Suppose, for example, that Gradley had been a senator before running for president and had a fairly liberal voting record on most issues. Here again, if a voter knew of this record, she would not take Gradley's median platform at face value. Rather, the voter's estimate of Gradley's true platform, or how the voter expects Gradley to behave in office, would be a combination of the promises contained in the platform and what was implied by these other sources of information.

Why don't candidates ignore these constraints—why can't Gradley proclaim, "I'm a different kind of Democrat, and plus I've changed my mind since I cast all those liberal votes." The problem is cheap talk. Why should rational voters believe a candidate whose platform is inconsistent with other information about how he is likely to behave in office? A candidate whose platform radically contradicts voters' expectations is unlikely to win office, simply because voters won't support someone who appears to be trying to mislead them.

In sum, platform choices are constrained by a candidate's record and other information that voters can use to determine how the candidate will behave if elected. Thus, a candidate may be forced to run on a nonmedian platform, because this choice reflects the electorate's expectations about how he will behave if elected.

Primary Elections. Up to now, the discussion here has focused on how candidates compete in general elections, ignoring the institutions that determine which candidates are allowed to participate in the contest. For most candidates in American elections, getting elected is a two-step process. First a candidate must gain her party's nomination by winning a primary election, then she competes in the general election.[7]

The fact that primary elections are used to select general election candidates has a profound impact on platform choices. Democratic primary electorates tend to be more liberal than the population as a whole, while Republican primary electorates tend to be more conservative. In other words, the ideal point of the median voter in the Democratic primary is somewhat to the left of the ideal point of the median voter in the general electorate. The median Republican's ideal point is similarly skewed to the right. Because of the difference between the primary and general election medians, a platform that maximizes a candidate's chances of winning a primary might not maximize her chances of winning the general election.

Why? Consider candidate McBush, a Republican. He maximizes his chances of winning his party's primary by choosing a platform that's close to the ideal point of the median Republican. But this platform is likely to be some distance away from the ideal point of the median voter in the general election and, thus, will not maximize McBush's chances of winning that election.

Conversely, if McBush focuses on the general election when choosing a platform and ignores the primary, he will probably choose a platform that matches the ideal point of the median voter in the general election. Unfortunately, this platform may be far away from the ideal point of the median voter in the primary and may put McBush at risk of losing the primary and not getting on the general election ballot in the first place.

---

[7]Candidates can also get on the general-election ballot by getting enough voters to sign nomination petitions, but in most states this option is very costly and time consuming, so it is almost always easier to gain access to the general-election ballot by competing in a primary.

Why doesn't McBush select one platform for the primary election and another for the general election? If he could, he would. However, once a candidate selects a platform, voters are likely to ignore attempts at repositioning, based on the expectation that the changes reflect political calculations, not a fundamental change in how the candidate will behave once elected.

Faced with electoral institutions that force them to compete in two elections with different electorates, candidates must choose: Do they focus on winning the primary election or the general election? Candidates who look ahead to the general election and choose a moderate platform are vulnerable to defeat by opponents who run on platforms that are optimal for winning the primary election. The presence of such opponents (or the expectation that they might enter the race) can lead rational candidates to ignore the general election entirely and choose a platform that's optimal for winning their party's nomination. As a result, these candidates are stuck with platforms that are not optimal for the purposes of winning the general election.

For example, consider the 1972 Democratic presidential primaries. George McGovern won the Democratic nomination for president, only to be soundly defeated by Republican Richard Nixon in the general election. It is almost surely true that some of the candidates McGovern defeated in the primaries (Edmund Muskie and Hubert Humphrey) would have had a better chance against Nixon. Why were these candidates defeated in the primaries? Their platforms were well suited to winning a general election but failed to attract support from primary voters. McGovern's platform was a better match to the preferences and demands of primary voters but was far away from what the median voter in the general election wanted.

Personal Policy Goals. A final reason why a candidate might ignore the "move to the median" advice has to do with his personal policy goals. The assumption that candidates only care about winning is useful for determining how electoral pressures shape platform choices. As a description of reality, however, this assumption is clearly too simple. It is surely true that most candidates want to win—why run if winning doesn't matter? But most candidates have policy preferences of their own, preferences they are unwilling to ignore when choosing a platform. As a result, their platforms may move away from the preferences held by the median voter in the primary and the general election, in favor of the policies that the candidates themselves prefer.

Barry Goldwater is a good example of how policy goals can shape a candidate's platform. In selecting a platform for the 1964 presidential campaign, Goldwater probably knew that he was advocating policies that the median voter would not like. There is no doubt that he hoped that his campaign would convert some voters to his way of thinking. But Goldwater had to know that a more moderate platform would have been a better choice for the purposes of winning the election. Why didn't he switch? Because he had strong ideas of what government should be doing, and was unwilling to compromise his views, even if running on an extreme platform reduced his chances of winning.

How often should you expect candidates to choose platforms that are far away from the median? Not very. Barry Goldwater is very much the exception in American politics. In general, candidates who consistently value policy over election don't survive very long. Either they never run in the first place, or they run and are defeated by candidates who hold moderate policy goals or who are willing to subordinate their policy concerns in favor of what the median voter wants.

Review of the Median Voter Theory

George Wallace was right. In many elections, there won't be a dime's worth of difference between the candidates. Wallace was wrong, however, in his diagnosis of why candidates look the same. The problem is not a conspiracy to deny voters a real choice. Nor is it a failure of honor or nerve. Rather, candidates move to the median out of a desire to win political office.

A voter might want candidates to differentiate themselves from each other. However, the goal of getting elected does not motivate candidates to behave this way. People who feel that candidates should offer distinct choices must remember what happened to Barry Goldwater in the presidential election of 1964: He presented a "real choice," but was crushed by Lyndon Johnson.

In other words, Wallace's Law comes with Goldwater's Caveat: The candidate who decides to create more than a dime's worth of difference risks losing the election. A candidate wins not by offering a choice, but by locating his platform right on top of the median voter, even if his platform echoes his opponent's.

Thus, how do elections and the need to attract votes shape candidates' promises? By creating an incentive for candidates to select platforms that are attractive to moderate voters. Many factors—personal policy preferences, primary elections, and credibility concerns—can limit the degree that a candidate is willing or able to move to the median. Even so, these factors do not negate the fact that moving to the median is a sure-fire way of winning an election.

Is this incentive a bad thing? Many critics attack the propensity of candidates to locate themselves in the "mushy center." For example, Jim Hightower, the former Agriculture Commissioner of Texas, was often heard to say, "the only things in the middle of the road are yellow lines and squashed armadillos." However, many of these critics (Hightower included) usually hold relatively extreme views on public policy. From their viewpoint, the fact that candidates are led to run on moderate platforms is a bad thing. But remember why the median is an attractive place for candidates: A majority of voters prefer a centrist candidate to one who is extreme. In other words, candidates move their platforms to the median because most voters like them to be there.

Of course, candidates move to the median not out of a sense of obligation, but because they fear that if they don't, they will be defeated by an opponent who does. Thus, if you want to ensure that a candidate selects a moderate platform rather than an extreme one, you have to make sure that she has an opponent in the next election and that the opponent is well funded and knows how to run a good campaign. Without a credible opponent (or no opponent at all), politicians do not face any sort of pressure to move toward the median.

Policy and Reelection. Finally, the median-voter theorem is often read as saying that politicians face a stark tradeoff: They can pursue policy or win office. That is, they can run on a platform that reflects their personal policy concerns, or they can choose a platform that is compatible with what the median voter wants. Deciding in favor of policy, it is said, dooms a politician to defeat by a candidate who is willing to take whatever positions are necessary to be elected.

This interpretation is also consistent with the widely held belief that politicians in America care too much about staying in office and too little about presenting voters with coherent, well thought out plans for solving national problems. Critics charge that members of Congress who care about enacting good public policies are vulnerable to opponents who are willing to say or do whatever is needed to get elected.

However, there are situations where a politician can run and win on a platform that reflects her policy concerns. In fact, many members of Congress argue that a large proportion of their colleagues do just that. One House member described the possibility this way.[8]

> I could take you down the hall and introduce you to a member who just drips his district, from his shoes to his straw hat. You don't have to go to his district to know what it's like; you just have to look at him. That's why the House is so great. It's a bunch of different cultures, all in different districts. If I went to Long Island with my record, they'd laugh me out. *Congress represents its districts because each member comes from his district much more so than because he tries to adapt his personal philosophy.*

In other words, some members of Congress can write their dream policy platform and get elected on it for the simple reason that their preferences are close to those held by their median constituent. For these lucky candidates, the spatial model's tradeoff between policy and reelection does not exist.

Thus, you should not conclude that elections are dominated by candidates who only care about getting reelected. On the contrary, the median voter theorem tells us that candidates who care about good public policy can run and win. The only requirement is that their policy goals be close to those held by the median voter in their districts.

How Constituents Make Trust Decisions

Why do voters trust elected representatives?[9] At first glance, this behavior is very puzzling. Intuitively, rational voters who care about what government does would reward their representative for casting votes that are consistent with their demands and punish her for voting against their demands. Trust short-circuits this mechanism. Constituents[10] who trust their representative are saying, in effect, "I will approve of your decision, regardless of how it looks to me." In other words, trust eliminates the incentives created by voter evaluations. With trust, a representative can act as she thinks best and ignore constituent demands.

---

[8]Bianco, *Trust*, p. 39.
[9]This section draws on Bianco, 1994.
[10]The term "constituents" means any registered voter in a representative's district.

Consider HR 3660, the Ethics Act of 1989. This measure was designed to increase congressional pay by about $30,000, a 25 percent increase. In addition, the act placed new ethics restrictions on members of Congress. Members could no longer receive outside income from law practices or other employment. The act also banned honoraria, or the practice of paying members for speaking at conferences, trade associations, or other organizations.

Suppose a legislator faces a vote on the Ethics Act. He wants to vote for the proposal but knows that his constituents strongly oppose the measure. Without trust, the legislator faces a stark choice: vote no, which will make constituents happy, or vote yes, in which case constituents will be upset and less likely to reelect him. It is as though constituents have told the legislator, "We don't want a pay raise—vote no, or else."

The situation is very different when constituents trust the representative. Now the legislator can vote for Ethics Act, knowing that constituents will approve of whatever he does. It is as though constituents have said, "While we oppose the pay raise, if you think it's a good idea, we will support a yea vote." Instead of worrying about what constituents want, the representative can focus on his feelings about the proposal—"Is it a good bill?"

The question is, why do voters trust elected officials? Put another way, why would rational voters decide to abandon their primary means of control over the actions of their representative?

The Ethics Act is a good place to look for answers to these questions. Using the language here, the average citizen prefers that all pay raises be defeated and demands that her representative vote against all such proposals. Even so, a majority of House members voted for the Ethics Act in late 1989. Moreover, in many districts, the majority of citizens appeared to be happy with their representative's support for this bill. It appears that in a large number of districts, constituents decided to let their representative act as she thought best on the Ethics Act—they decided to trust their representative's judgment about the proposal.

Why would rational constituents opt against trying to control their representative's behavior? This section shows that trust can be a rational choice. In particular, trust makes sense when constituents believe that their representative knows things about proposals that they do not and that their representative's interests are compatible with their own.

How Do Voters Evaluate Elected Representatives?

Why do constituents face decisions about trust? The answer lies in how they evaluate their legislator's performance in office and in the information—or lack of information—they bring to these evaluations.

Retrospective Evaluations. Scholars of American politics believe that constituents monitor their representative's behavior, rewarding actions that they believe to be consistent with their interests and punishing actions that appear to be contrary.[11] The "reward" is a more positive evaluation of the incumbent's performance, making the voter more likely to support the incumbent in the next election. "Punishment" is a more negative evaluation, making future votes for the incumbent less likely.

Political scientists label these judgments *retrospective evaluations,* retrospective because they occur after the representative acts. However, representatives anticipate their constituents' reactions when deciding what to do. That is, faced with two courses of action, an incumbent asks, how will my constituents respond to these actions? Which ones will they approve of? Which ones will make them angry?

In making these judgments, the incumbent is not concerned with his constituents' happiness per se. Rather, he is calculating the political consequences of different actions—whether doing one thing rather than another increases or decreases his probability of reelection.

Votes decisions are a good example. Suppose an incumbent faces a vote on the Ethics Act and knows that her constituents oppose the measure. Without trust, a yea vote is politically costly. Constituents will evaluate it unfavorably and be somewhat less likely to support the incumbent in the future. A nay vote, on the other hand, will trigger positive evaluations and increase the incumbent's chances of reelection.

When politicians care about getting reelected, retrospective evaluations can have a profound impact on their behavior. Simply put, if a politician's desire to be reelected is strong enough, he will take actions that are consistent with what constituents want, which will guarantee that constituents make positive evaluations and cement

---

[11]Such monitoring occurs on a small fraction of the proposals that members of Congress vote on—the ones that most citizens care about, such as votes on social issues like abortion, taxation, and, of course, pay raises for elected officials.

their support in the next election. In the example here, insofar as the legislator wants to be reelected, he will comply with constituent demands and vote against the proposal.

The Problem: Policy Uncertainty. The problem with retrospective evaluations is that they give representatives the right incentives—to act in accordance with their constituents' interests—only if constituents are well informed about the details of legislation. Unfortunately, as discussed in Chapter Four, the average constituent knows very little about the things that members of Congress vote on. That is, constituents often operate under a condition of *policy uncertainty.* Either they don't know whether their interests are best served by enacting or defeating a proposal or, worse yet, they are misinformed about which result is best.

Policy uncertainty can have dire consequences for retrospective evaluations. Constituents who are unsure or misinformed about a proposal may place the wrong sort of demands on their representative. They may demand a yea vote when defeating the proposal is actually better for them or demand a nay vote when enacting the proposal makes them better off. If their representative complies with these sorts of demands, her votes will receive favorable evaluations even though they are contrary to constituent interests.

Consider the Ethics Act. Suppose that constituents don't know about the ethics reforms in the act and see it as just a pay raise. If they knew about the ethics provisions, they might well support the act and demand that their representative vote yea. But since they are misinformed and believe that the only thing the Ethics Act will do is raise congressional pay, they will demand a vote against the proposal. If their representative complies with this demand, his vote will be exactly what constituents asked for, but it will also be contrary to their interests.

This problem doesn't go away if a representative decides to ignore political consequences and simply "do the right thing" for her constituents. Such acts of political courage will cost political support and may even result in the representative being thrown out of office—all for trying to do right by her constituents.

How Does Trust Work?

Trust exists when constituents evaluate (or are prepared to evaluate) their representative's vote positively, regardless of whether they believe that the vote is consistent with their interests. In other words, trust allows a representative to act as he thinks best without worrying that his actions will cost him political support.

Conversely, trust does not exist when constituents issue (or are prepared to issue) a favorable evaluation only if their representative complies with their demands—does what they want. Under these conditions, a representative must implement constituent demands to maintain or increase her chances of reelection.

Why Trust? The rationale for trust is simple: Compared to the average constituent, the average representative has better information about legislative proposals. Legislators get this information from hearings and floor debates, committee reports, caucus proceedings, and personal staff.

Think about the Ethics Act. What are its effects? It will certainly increase congressional pay. In addition, the ethics provisions will, in theory, reduce the influence of special interests in the policy process and eliminate potential conflicts of interest, thereby strengthening the link between representatives and voters. In the worst case, the act would have no effect on responsiveness or ethics and simply give legislators a pay raise.

This description of the Ethics Act illustrates why legislators might know things their constituents do not. Only members know the extent to which special interests can get what they want (access to members or staff, small changes to policy proposals, etc.) by offering honoraria. Only members know whether their ability to collect outside income leads to conflicts of interest. Constituents may have some idea of these problems, but they will know less than their representatives do.

This difference in information levels between legislators and their constituents creates a clear rationale for trust. By allowing a representative to use her judgment, constituents ensure that the representative's decision will be based on her superior understanding of choices and their consequences rather than on the limited information available to constituents.

The Problem with Trust: Control. Representatives like trust a lot. It enables them to do what they think is right rather than doing what their constituents want. Even if a representative is prepared to ignore his constituents' demands, trust lowers the political costs of going his own way.

For constituents, however, decisions about trust are problematic. With trust, representatives can ignore the misinformed, half-baked demands of their constituents and choose based on their superior information. However, trust also allows a representative to disregard *all* demands, not just the half-baked ones. Put another way, trust allows a representative to do what she thinks best, even if the results are bad for her constituents.

Think about the Ethics Act. Suppose that constituents favor enacting the bill if it really will produce a more ethical Congress, but want it defeated if it will only raise pay. Suppose the representative knows that the ethics provisions will have no effect but wants a raise. Given trust, the representative can vote for the bill, knowing that his constituents will see this action and think, "Well, we were suspicious about the Ethics Act, but since our representative voted for it, the bill must do good things for congressional ethics. Thank goodness we allowed our representative to use his judgment."

In sum, while constituents want a representative they can trust, they have to worry about whether they should trust the one they have. The next section considers what factors rational constituents would consider when making trust decisions.

How Do Rational Constituents Make Trust Decisions?

This section describes how rational constituents make trust decisions. As you will see, trust hinges on two factors: how much constituents know about the proposal being voted on (*policy uncertainty*) and what they know about their representative's policy preferences (*common interest*). Constituents who are unsure of a proposal's effects and who believe their representative wants the same things they do will generally decide in favor of trust. Conversely, constituents who think they know a lot about a proposal or who believe their representative's policy preferences differ from their own will generally decide against trust.

Why No Explanations? Before describing where trust comes from, it is important to understand what doesn't create trust: a representative's explanations of her behavior. Members of Congress spend a lot of time telling constituents why they did what they did. They offer these explanations during face-to-face interactions, such as speeches or question-and-answer sessions with constituents, and through indirect means, such as media coverage or newsletters.

Why not talk about the role of explanations in creating trust? *Because members of Congress don't think that trust comes from explanations.* When this author put the question to House incumbents, most dismissed the idea as a foolish academic notion, completely out of touch with real-world politics. Members of Congress expect to be asked about their behavior and always offer reasons for their votes, but they do not believe that their responses build trust.

One reason is the problem of getting a message out to constituents. The term *explaining* suggests a forum where constituents assemble to hear their representative. However, districts contain many people, often scattered across a large area. Even with a maximum effort—sending out newsletters, aggressively courting print and electronic media, speaking before every group who will listen—only a minority of constituents are likely to see or hear an explanation.

Moreover, contact is only the first step in creating trust. Constituents also have to believe what they are told. Why should they? After all, explanations look a lot like cheap talk. And as you saw in Chapter Four, rational voters often have good reason to ignore cheap talk. Thus, regardless of how much a legislator would like to explain her behavior, she has to contend with the fact that her messages often fall on deaf ears.

Why Trust: Policy Uncertainty. When evaluating their representative's behavior, constituents generally face *policy uncertainty.* That is, they don't know whether enacting the proposal will help them or hurt them. The level of policy uncertainty varies across proposals. Sometimes constituents believe that they know a lot about a proposal's effects (low uncertainty), and sometimes they think they know very little (high uncertainty).

Policy uncertainty is a necessary condition for trust. If constituents know or think they know what a proposal will do, they have no reason to defer to a legislator's judgments. Why let someone else choose for you when you know as much as they do? If you know that enacting the proposal makes you better off, you should demand that your representative vote for it. If you are sure that defeat produces a better outcome, you should demand a nay vote.

However, if you're not sure what a proposal might do, demanding that your representative vote yea (or nay) may produce a bad result. You may force the legislator to vote yea when defeat is better, given your interests. Or you may demand a nay vote when you would be better off if the proposal was enacted. In sum, if you are unsure of what a proposal will do, it makes sense for you to think about trusting your representative as a way of substituting her well-informed perceptions for your uncertainty.

The impact of different levels of policy uncertainty is easy to understand. Constituents who have low uncertainty are relatively sure of the outcome they will get from enacting a proposal. In the case of the Ethics Act, for example, these voters are sure (or almost sure) that the proposal is just a pay raise or that it really is a pay and ethics package. At the other extreme are constituents with high uncertainty, who find it hard to predict what the proposal will do if enacted: That is, they're not sure whether the act would raise pay and improve ethics, or just raise pay.

Constituents with low uncertainty are unlikely to trust their representative. This response makes sense if you remember what trust is supposed to do. Constituents trust their representative because they believe that he knows more about a proposal than they do. As policy uncertainty declines, there is less and less of a reason for a constituent to defer to her representative's judgment—the value of the representative's expertise declines because the constituent is becoming an expert herself.

Conversely, as a constituent's policy uncertainty increases, meaning that he knows less and less about a proposal's effects, trust should become more likely. In other words, if we compare two constituents, one who says, "The Ethics Act is just a pay raise," and the other who says, "The Ethics Act is too complicated for me, who knows what it will do?" the second constituent should be more likely to trust his representative.

Why Trust: Common Interest. Certainty is only part of the trust equation, however. The second critical factor in trust decisions is what constituents think about their representative's policy preferences. Faced with a decision about trust, a rational constituent will ask, "If I allow my representative to use her judgment, how likely is it that the resulting vote will be consistent with my interests?" In other words, in order to decide about trust, constituents must calculate the likelihood of a *common interest.*[12]

To illustrate what "common interest" means, suppose that your representative is going to vote on the Ethics Act, and you have to decide whether to trust her judgment. Your preferences are simple: A proposal that raises pay and improves ethics is worth enacting, but a

---

[12]The next section shows how constituents make judgments about common interest.

proposal that just raises pay should be defeated. The question you must consider is, do your representative's preferences look like your own, or would she favor the proposal even if its only effect will be to give House members a pay raise?

To say that your representative's preferences are identical to your own means that she wants to vote for the Ethics Act only if she knows that the proposal both raises pay and improves ethics and prefers to vote against the proposal if it raises pay but has no impact on ethics. If the representative's preferences match this description, then you have a common interest with the representative and you should trust her judgment.

Now consider the other possibility. Suppose your representative would be happy to vote for the Ethics Act even if the ethics reforms won't do anything. These preferences don't match your own. Under these conditions, no common interest exists and you should decide against trust.

The concept of common interest captures exactly what rational constituents should worry about when making decisions about trust. Simply put, if they let their representative act as a free agent, what are the chances that he will act in their interest? When a common interest exists, a representative and his constituents agree whether a proposal should be enacted or defeated. Under these conditions, a representative can be trusted to act in the interests of his constituents—not out of altruism, but because the representative's motivations are such that he will do exactly what constituents would do, if they knew what the representative knows.

Summary. Rational constituents are more likely to trust their representative insofar as they are uncertain about a proposal's effects and believe that there is a good chance that they have a common interest with their representative. If rational constituents believe that a common interest does not exist, then they will decide against trust, even if they know very little about a proposal. And if they are extremely confident in their judgments about a proposal, they will also refuse to trust their representative, unless the likelihood of a common interest is extremely high.

Are Real-World Constituents Rational About Trust?

Having learned how a rational constituent would make trust decisions, you are probably wondering whether real-world constituents come close to this standard of behavior. This section examines trust decisions involving the Ethics Act. You will see that policy uncertainty and beliefs about common interest played a critical role in generating trust on this proposal.

Moreover, consistent with the discussion in Chapter Four, voters' beliefs about common interest came from information about their representative's personal characteristics. Trust was associated with attributes such as a member's personal wealth, a record of earning substantial honoraria or outside income, or actions such as refusing to accept the raise mandated by the Ethics Act.

The quotes presented here were gathered through interviews with members of the U.S. House of Representatives. Members were asked about their constituents' feelings about the Ethics Act, their personal feelings about the proposal, and whether they believed that constituents trusted their judgments about the act.

Policy Uncertainty. Based on the interviews, districts were divided into three groups, strong opposition, opposition, and weak support. (There were no strong-support districts.) Constituents in strong-opposition districts generally favored defeat of the Ethics Act and were nearly certain that this outcome was consistent with their policy preferences. For these constituents, the act was a pay raise, nothing more.

In opposition districts, constituents also opposed the Ethics Act, but their feelings were much less intense than in strong-opposition districts. They would support a bill that raised pay and improved congressional ethics but would oppose a bill that just raised pay. Finally, constituents in weak-support districts either favored raising congressional pay, thought the ethics provisions in the act would have a significant effect, or were unsure of what the proposal would do.

How did these beliefs influence trust decisions? Representatives elected from strong-opposition districts almost never reported trust on the Ethics Act. This finding is no surprise: Constituents in these districts were virtually certain that the act was just a pay raise and opposed it on that basis.

At the other extreme, all of the representatives from weak-support districts reported trust. Again, this reaction is no surprise. Constituents in these districts were either highly unsure what the act would do or favored the idea of raising congressional pay.

Most congressional districts fell into the middle category—opposition. Constituents in these districts generally held unfavorable opinions of the Ethics Act. However, their opposition was conditional: They would accept a yea vote if they thought their representative had a good reason for doing so—some reason that made the vote consistent with their interests. In particular, these constituents would favor a pay raise bill that also implemented real ethics reforms. For these constituents, trust was an open question. Their decision hinged on beliefs about common interest.

Perceptions of Common Interest. Constituents making a trust decision involving the Ethics Act must ask, "Would our representative support the Ethics Act if it's just a pay raise, or would she only support it if the measure improved ethics as well as raised pay?" Put another way, a representative will gain trust on the Ethics Act only if there's some indication that she doesn't want a pay raise, wouldn't get a raise out of the proposal, or wouldn't vote for the proposal unless it improved ethics as well as raised pay.

How would constituents answer this question about common interest? Chapter Four suggests that constituents will use what they know about their representative's background and personality to determine the representative's feelings about the Ethics Act. In particular, interviews with House members suggest that constituents believed that common interests were likely if their representative had one of three characteristics:

- personal wealth
- substantial honoraria (money earned from speeches) or outside income (earnings from a job outside Congress, such as a part-time law practice)
- refusal of the raise

Each of these characteristics will be discussed in turn to show how they influenced beliefs about common interest.

Wealth. A member's personal wealth had the clearest impact on perceptions of common interest and beliefs about trust. Simply put, constituents believed that wealthy legislators were focused on the ethics provisions contained in the act because they had less need of a raise. As one Southern Democrat explained,

> . . . for me, a vote for the pay raise is unselfish because I didn't need it. If a thirty-thousand dollar raise could become a campaign issue, it's not

worth it for me in political terms to vote for it. . . . It's pretty well known that I have the second-largest net worth in the delegation. Some of my constituents don't like that I was born with a silver spoon in my mouth, but the others just think it's harder to buy me.

In other words, if a wealthy legislator voted for the Ethics Act, his constituents would say something like, "He didn't vote for the Ethics Act because he wanted a raise—he doesn't need one. He must have voted yea because he thought the ethics reforms would do some good."

Honoraria and Outside Income. A second factor that led constituents in opposition districts to conclude that they had common interests with their representative was if the representative had a record of accepting substantial honoraria or had large amounts of outside income. One of the Ethics Act's major reforms was to prevent members from accepting honoraria and to ban almost all types of outside income. Consequently, a substantial fraction of the House, those with substantial honoraria and outside income, received at best a trivial increase in pay because of the act's passage.

Members who wouldn't get a raise from the act because their loss of honoraria and outside income would negate it tended to report high levels of trust. As one incumbent noted,

> I got hit hard by the bill because I practice law. I'm still a senior partner in a firm with fifty members. Last year I got a check for thirty thousand from that, but I'll have to resign December 31st because of the ethics reforms. So the bill hurt me more than other members. . . . I could have voted for the raise with impunity.

This member believed his constituents would reason as follows: "We know that our representative lost all that outside income because of the Ethics Act, so he couldn't have supported the bill just to get a raise. He must have voted yea because he thought the ethics reforms were a good idea."

Refusal of the Raise. Finally, some representatives argued that refusing to accept the raise contained in the Ethics Act would generate trust. As one opponent of the act said,

> If I had believed that the ethics reforms were important, I could have voted for the package and told folks that I didn't agree with the raise and

didn't take the money, but that the other reforms were critical because Washington's become corrupted with outside interests. That would couple a yes vote with a refusal to take the money.

This representative believed that refusing the raise would signal a common interest with his constituents. With the raise removed as a motive, constituents would infer that he voted yea in order to improve congressional ethics. As it happened, this representative didn't vote for the act because he thought the ethics reforms didn't go far enough. But he believed that if he had voted for the proposal, constituents would have trusted his judgment and evaluated his vote favorably.

What happened to representatives who didn't have one of these characteristics? In general, they weren't trusted. For some of them, the lack of trust wasn't a problem: They opposed the act themselves, so they were happy to vote as their constituents demanded. However, supporters of the act who faced constituent opposition and who didn't expect trust had an unhappy choice: vote yea and make constituents angry, or vote nay against a bill they favored.

In sum, analysis of the Ethics Act shows that trust decisions are driven by policy uncertainty and beliefs about common interest. A substantial number of representatives—those with the right characteristics—were free to vote as they thought best. A few were lucky enough to represent districts where constituents themselves favored the act. And the remaining legislators, those who could not signal that they shared constituent interests or who represented strong opposition districts, generally did not expect or receive trust on this proposal.

Trust and Rationality: A Summary

Trust decisions are rational choices. Trust does not arise because constituents are unable to think for themselves. It doesn't happen because representatives can hoodwink or hypnotize constituents into accepting whatever they do. Rather, trust occurs because constituents want to tap their representative's private information and expertise. And constituents make this choice only when they believe that it improves the chances of achieving the outcomes they want.

The analysis here also shows that seemingly irrational trust decisions can in fact be smart behavior. For example, rational, sensible constituents may refuse to trust their representative even when they know very little and are sure that she is an expert. Results such as these suggest that many times when constituents appear to make bizarre decisions about trust, the reason lies in what they know (or think they know) about the proposal and about their representative not in their inability to make good trust decisions.

The analysis also shows that constituents may make mistakes about trust. They may refuse to defer in situations where a common interest exists but their legislator doesn't have the characteristics needed to signal this agreement. They may decide to trust their representative in situations where a common interest doesn't exist. To say that these mistakes are possible does not imply that voters are unwilling or unable to be rational. It simply means that they choose under conditions of uncertainty.

Moreover, it appears that some representatives will be trusted more than others—those who have characteristics that suggest they agree with their constituents on a wide range of issues. A luckless few representatives will not have any of these characteristics. For them, trust will be a rare thing indeed. This variation in trust does not arise because some constituents are smarter than others or because some representatives are better than others at pulling the wool over their constituents' eyes. Rather, it is driven by variations in what representatives look like to their constituents.

Finally, this discussion shows that the link between representatives and their constituents is fundamentally imperfect. If constituents had good information about legislative proposals, it would be easy to ensure that their representatives acted in accordance with their interests. All constituents would need to do is make their interests known to their representatives, who would vote in accordance with these interests or risk being thrown out of office.

In the real world, where constituents often are uncertain or misinformed, representation does not fit this neat description. Trust provides a partial remedy to constituent uncertainty. Even then, constituents will sometimes make mistakes, either refusing to trust their representative when they should or deciding in favor of trust when they should not. But these failures are not the result of irrationality or indifference. Rather, they arise because constituents make trust decisions under conditions of uncertainty.

Summary

Why do candidates for the same office often sound the same? Why do constituents trust elected officials? At first glance, both of these phenomena suggest that something is wrong with the average voter. Why would a voter reward candidates for sounding the same or throw away their influence over the actions of elected officials?

This chapter has shown that both phenomena can be explained as the consequence of rational choices. Voters don't think about getting candidates to move to the median. But the calculations that drive their votes create a strong incentive for candidates to behave in this way. A voter prefers a candidate whose platform lies close to her ideal point. Faced with an electorate of voters who think in this way, candidates increase their chances of winning elections by moving their platforms as close as they can to the median voter's ideal point. Thus, the lack of a real choice that's often observed in American elections is not so much the fault of candidates as it is a consequence of how citizens make vote decisions.

Similarly, this chapter has also shown that it can sometimes be rational for voters to allow their representative to act as a free agent. However, such trust is not automatic. Representatives have discretion and are allowed to use their judgment only when voters believe that by doing so they will be better off—in other words, when voters believe they and their representatives share the same policy outcome preferences.

~ 6 ~

Strategic Behavior in Congress

S trategic behavior in Congress falls into two broad categories: choices involving the writing and enacting of legislation and choices that set up congressional rules and institutions. This chapter considers one example from each category.

The first section focuses on distributive proposals—legislation that funds the construction of roads, buildings, and other projects. These proposals are often described as wasteful—spending government money on projects that are of little use to anyone. If so, why do rational legislators work so hard to expand the size of these proposals and to ensure they are enacted? And why do rational constituents reward representatives for behaving in this way?

Consider the 1998 Transportation Equity Act for the 21st Century ("TEA-21"), which funded over $250 billion worth of road projects. One observer described the proposal as "tasty highway pork," a "pork-filled, election-year plum for members of Congress."[1] The implication is that many of the projects in TEA-21 simply aren't worth

[1]Rick Henderson, "Tasty Highway Pork," *Journal of Commerce* 18 March 1997, p. 6A.

building—the benefits are less than the costs. Yet an overwhelming majority of House members and senators voted for the proposal. Their constituents were happy to see the program enacted. Why do so many approve of a proposal that wastes taxpayer money? What's the rational-choice explanation for this behavior?

This chapter shows that legislators favor distributive proposals because delivering these benefits to constituents increases their chances of reelection. Expanding distributive proposals ensures that every legislator who wants to claim credit has the opportunity to do so. And constituents support their representative's efforts because if they don't, pork-barrel proposals will still be enacted but without providing anything to them.

The second part of the chapter focuses on an important congressional institution, the committee system. The aim is to explain *committee deference*: why rational legislators let committee members dominate the legislative process for proposals within their committee's jurisdiction.

Consider the House Science Committee. Committee members are seen as experts, as a source of information and advice to colleagues not on the committee. And when the Science Committee reports a proposal to the floor of the House of Representatives, members will typically enact the proposal with little or no debate.

Why do House members allow their colleagues on committees to decide things for them? It would seem there could be a danger in enabling committee members to make policy decisions the way they want to, since these decisions could be inconsistent with what noncommittee legislators would like to do. Why would rational legislators give away their power to make decisions?

This chapter shows that there are two answers to this question. In some cases, deference is a way for legislators to implement a trade or deal, where they allow colleagues on other committees to act as they see fit in return for the same authority when their own committee considers a proposal. This explanation is most relevant for the typical congressional committee—such as the House Science Committee—that deals with issues that few members consider important.

On committees that deal with highly salient, controversial proposals, deference is a way for committee members to share their expertise and information with their colleagues. Such deference occurs only because members are assigned to high-salience committees with this information-sharing goal in mind. In other words, rational legislators defer to the members of high-salience committees because these groups were deliberately constructed to function as information sources for the rest of Congress.

Distributive Politics and Rational Legislators

Distributive proposals spend federal tax revenue on projects that benefit specific towns, cities, or localities. Examples include spending on highways, water treatment plants, parks, and other public works. These proposals are often labeled *pork barrel* projects and are seen as a wasteful, inferior way to spend government money.

Just about everything the federal government does can be shoehorned into a distributive proposal. For example, bureaucrats in the National Aeronautics and Space Administration (NASA) are famous for making sure that their major projects use components produced in all fifty states. Accordingly, NASA's new space station is often referred to as the "orbiting pork barrel."

Pork-barrel programs are the kind of appropriation that gets mentioned on talk radio or by television comedians, and for good reason—they often seem downright silly. Consider a 1998 appropriation that gave $3.3 million for studies of shrimp raising studies in Hawaii, Mississippi, Massachusetts, California, and *Arizona*. This project drew a reasonable question from Senator John McCain: "I have yet to fathom the logic of conducting shrimp research in the desert."[2]

Moreover, the pursuit of pork isn't limited to the U.S. Congress. As Nikita Khrushchev, the General Secretary of the Soviet Union during the 1950s and 1960s, is alleged to have once said, "Politicians are the same all over. They promise to build bridges even when there are no rivers."

The first step in understanding why so much distributive legislation gets enacted is to determine why rational legislators would want to enact wasteful pork-barrel bills and why rational constituents would reward them for this behavior.

As you will see, these bills are enacted because they help legislators get reelected—they are part of a legislator's answer when con-

[2]Jim Drinkard, "Congress' 'Pork Barrel Politics' Leaves Gifts to Benefit States Before Closing '97 Session" *Sun Herald Online*, 1997. http://www.sunherald.com/region/docs/pork1124.htm

stituents ask, "What have you done for us lately?" Moreover, rational constituents will reward elected officials for delivering pork-barrel projects, even if they know that the costs of these projects outweigh their benefits.

This section also explains the structure of distributive proposals. In general, pork-barrel bills supply benefits to as many congressional districts as possible. This pattern is surprising. Intuitively, once benefits have been supplied to a majority of districts, the authors should be able to relax, knowing that a majority of members will vote for the proposal and thereby enact it. Why then do rational legislators favor *Christmas tree bills*, proposals that have "something for everyone," when a smaller, less-expensive (or less-wasteful) proposal could easily be enacted?

What Does the Pork Barrel Look Like?

Distributive proposals fund all sorts of projects, from roads to space stations to outhouses to shrimp research. TEA-21 is a good example.[3] Most—over 90 percent—of the $270 billion allocated by the act is distributed to states based on population and other factors. However, over $18 billion were given out for specific highway, mass transit, bridge, bike path, and economic development projects.

Some of the projects funded by TEA-21 appear quite reasonable, even if you're skeptical about the merits of distributive legislation:

- $24 million to fix a sixty-one-year old bridge in northwestern Vermont
- $5.8 million for new traffic signals in Compton, California
- $26 million for construction of an Interstate 95 interchange in New Haven, Connecticut

Fixing bridges, upgrading stoplights, and building highway exits all seem like worthy expenditures. People may disagree about whether these projects constitute the best use of government funds, but there is little doubt that the improvements create real benefits.

However, some of the other projects in TEA-21 have little or

---

[3]The bill was originally called the Building Efficient Surface Transportation and Equity Act. The description of TEA-21 was drawn from Eric Pianin and Charles R. Babcock, "Highway Earmarks Hold Record Pork," *Washington Post*, April 1, 1998, p. A1, and Jonathan Cohn, "Roll Out the Barrel," *The New Republic*, April 20, 1998, p. 19.

nothing to do with the task of meeting America's transportation needs. Consider these four:

- $1.6 million for the Missouri Botanical Garden
- $3 million for research into spinal-cord injuries
- $3 million for a documentary on "infrastructure awareness"
- $500,000 for a study of how to improve access to the Kennedy Center for the Performing Arts

News accounts also noted that TEA-21 contained over 130 projects for Pennsylvania, the home state of Representative Bud Shuster, the "Prince of Pork," who is chairman of the Transportation Committee. Shuster was also responsible for adding the Kennedy Center funding—he's on the center's board of directors.

Distributive proposals like TEA-21 come in many forms but have two things in common. First, a voter benefits only if the distributive proposal funds a project near where the voter lives. Only people who live in Compton will appreciate the new traffic signals funded by TEA-21, just as only the residents of northwestern Vermont will be happy with their bridge. If you live somewhere else, you won't know about the project, and if you do know about it, you won't care.

The second important fact about distributive proposals is that a legislator's support is generally tied to whether the measure provides something for her district.[4] Think about TEA-21. Unless a member of Congress likes to take long road trips or unless there's a long-haul transport firm in her district, the only reason she would support the proposal is if it contains something for her district. If it does, then the legislator will vote for the proposal as a way of securing benefits for her constituents. If, however, the proposal gives nothing to the legislator's district, she probably will oppose it.

Theories of Distributive Politics: Minimum Winning Coalitions and Universalism

How will rational legislators construct a distributive proposal? This section describes two possible answers. The first is that these propos-

---

[4]A few members of Congress oppose all distributive proposals, believing they are a waste of government money. Some of these legislators find other ways to claim credit or otherwise keep their constituents happy. Others are defeated by challengers who promise to deliver more benefits to the district.

als will deliver benefits to a bare majority of legislators—to a *minimum winning coalition*.[5] The second answer, *universalism*, states that distributive proposals will supply benefits to as many districts as possible, with no attempt to limit the size or the cost of the proposal.

Why should you worry about minimum winning coalitions and universalism? Because these concepts explain both why rational legislators would want to enact distributive proposals even when costs exceed benefits and why they would prefer to supply benefits to everyone rather than to a narrow majority.

Minimum Winning Coalitions. The theory of minimum winning coalitions states that in a legislature that enacts proposals using majority rule, the authors of a proposal should aim at attracting support from only a bare majority of legislators—no more and no less. Put another way, distributive proposals should be designed to deliver benefits to exactly a majority of districts.

Suppose you're a member of the House and want to enact TEA-21. You need to convince a majority of your colleagues to vote for the proposal. How can you do that? Remember that some legislators are unalterably opposed to the proposal, but that most legislators will vote yea if the proposal contains something for their district and oppose it otherwise. Therefore, your task is simple. Don't give anything to the unmovable opponents, and give enough projects to the remaining legislators such that exactly a majority of the House gets a project. If you follow this strategy, a majority of legislators (those representing districts that get projects) will vote for the proposal, and it will be enacted.

Do you need additional votes beyond a majority? No. Once TEA-21 has majority support, it will be enacted regardless of what the rest of the legislature does. You could increase support for the proposal by adding projects that benefit additional districts. But why bother? You already have a majority. Moreover, adding projects only increases the total cost of the proposal.

The logic of minimum winning coalitions can be understood by considering the problem of dividing a pie. Suppose you are a member of a group of seven people and are given the responsibility of dividing

[5]William H. Riker, *The Theory of Political Coalitions* (New Haven: Yale University Press, 1957).

a tasty pie into some number of equal-sized slices. Everyone in your group likes pie and wants as large a slice as possible. Since you are the slicer, you get a slice for sure and can distribute additional slices to as many other group members as you want. However, the members of the group must approve your slicing plan using majority rule.

How many slices will you offer to cut? The answer is, exactly four. This allocation allows you to get a piece and gives a slice to three other group members whom you have named. This plan will receive four votes, one from each person who receives a slice.

Why not fewer slices? Doing so gives you a bigger piece, but no such plan will receive majority support. (For example, a three-slice allocation garners three votes.)

Why not more slices? You could cut the pie into five, six, seven, or more slices. However, these strategies give you a smaller piece than you would receive from cutting only four slices, plus you don't need the additional votes that the new slices will attract.

In short, a four-slice division is the choice that gives you the largest piece and at the same time receives enough votes to be enacted. And in a seven-person group using majority rule, four people are a minimum winning coalition.

From this perspective, distributive proposals are a lot like pies. The theory predicts that they will be enacted by minimum winning coalitions. The districts of legislators inside the coalition will receive projects and pay a share of the costs. These legislators will vote for the bill. Districts of legislators outside the coalition will pay some costs but get no projects. They will oppose the proposal, either because they don't like distributive proposals or because their district didn't get a project.

Universalism. The problem with predicting that distributive proposals will be enacted by minimum wining coalitions is that the theory doesn't match reality. On the contrary, legislators who write distributive proposals try to deliver benefits to as many districts as possible, even if they must increase the cost of the program to do so. Political scientists use the term *universalism* to describe this practice.

Consider the TEA-21 highway bill. This bill supplied projects to over 400 of the 435 districts in the House of Representatives. In other words, more than 90 percent of House members could find something in the bill that they could claim credit for.

Why do members prefer universalism to minimum winning coalitions? Remember what a distributive proposal does. It spends money to build roads, water treatment plants, and other things. Put another way, distributive proposals create opportunities for *credit claiming*.[6] A member whose districts get benefits can go home and tell his constituents that he was responsible for getting these projects into the bill. Such credit claiming increases constituents' evaluations of their member's performance in office and thereby increases the member's chances of reelection.

Consider TEA-21, which, among other things, funded new traffic signals in Compton, California. After this project was completed, the representative from Compton probably went home to his or her district, held a town meeting underneath the new traffic lights, and said, "Aren't those new lights great? I made sure that members of the Transportation Committee knew we needed them." These claims get the member's name and picture in the paper—and give his or her constituents another reason to keep him or her in office.

The important thing to remember is that a member's ability to claim credit has nothing to do with how many of her colleagues are also able to do so. The only question is, does a distributive proposal deliver something that the member's constituents want? If it does, the member will be able to claim credit, regardless of how many of her colleagues can do the same.

That is, the representative from Compton can claim credit for traffic lights, the representative from Vermont can talk about the new bridge, and everyone else can take responsibility for the projects in their own districts—all without contradicting each other.

The fact that members evaluate distributive proposals in terms of credit claiming means they have a clear preference for universalism. Why not try to help everyone—that is, add money for spinal-cord research, documentaries on infrastructure awareness, and the Missouri Botanical Gardens? Doing so increases the proposal's cost because more projects will be funded. But if a member evaluates a distributive proposal in terms of whether it gives him or her something to claim credit for, the total cost of the proposal doesn't matter; the only question is whether it provides something for the member's district. If it does, then the member will support the proposal.

To put it another way, constructing a pork-barrel bill isn't like cutting a pie, where giving slices to additional people reduces the size of

---

[6]David Mayhew, *Congress: The Electoral Connection* (New Haven: Yale University Press, 1974).

your own piece. Rather, the key feature of pork-barrel proposals is that they provide opportunities for everyone to claim credit where one member's ability to claim credit doesn't in any way reduce his or her colleagues from doing so.

Following a universalistic norm has an additional benefit: It defuses opposition. Suppose the authors of a distributive proposal only included proposals for a minimum winning coalition of legislators. A minimum winning coalition is enough to enact the proposal, assuming all recipients vote yea. But some of the recipients may oppose distributive proposals regardless of whether they provide benefits to their districts. And a determined minority of legislators, particularly in the Senate, can make speeches and use other tactics to delay enactment of the bill. More importantly, opponents can hold press conferences and use other means to describe the proposal as yet another example of wasteful government spending.

Expanding the size of distributive proposals by providing benefits to as many legislators as possible is a good way of minimizing the number of legislators who might use these delaying or publicity tactics. Universalism expands the number of legislators who have good reason to want the proposal enacted so they can claim credit. With these benefits in hand, the new recipients have no reason to fight against passage of the proposal or to criticize it as wasteful government spending. Thus, legislators interested in credit claiming have no reason to oppose universalism and good reason to support it.

Again, consider TEA-21. It may have been tasty highway pork, but it passed in the House by a vote of 337–80 and in the Senate by 88–5. As these vote totals suggest, most members of Congress will vote for a distributive proposal that is laden with projects of dubious merit so long as it provides something for their district.

Why Constituents Reward the Provision of Pork. The last section explained why members of Congress prefer universalism to minimum winning coalitions—why they prefer a version of TEA-21 that contains a project for everyone who asks, rather than a smaller bill that only funds projects whose benefits exceed their costs or a proposal that only gives projects to a minimum winning coalition.

But what about constituents? Members like universalism because it ensures that they can claim credit. But this preference is only part of the explanation of pork-barrel bills. Legislators can only claim credit when constituents are happy with what they receive. Why do constituents reward their representative for getting them a project, when they have to swallow paying for the rest of the distributive proposal?

The citizens of Compton, California, for example, got new traffic lights because of TEA-21. But TEA-21 also funded projects across the rest of the country, including many of dubious worth. If you added up the costs and benefits of TEA-21 to the taxpayers of Compton, there's a good chance that they paid more than they received. If so, why was their representative able to claim credit?

Understanding the answer to this question is crucial to explaining why legislators prefer universalism, why distributive proposals get so big, and why no one cares when a project's costs exceed its benefits.

One explanation is that voters are misinformed about the benefits and costs of distributive proposals. The citizens of Compton, for example, have a good idea of the benefits from TEA-21: They see the new traffic lights that the proposal paid for. However, the cost of the proposal is buried in their annual income tax payment.

Under these conditions, it's easy to see how these constituents might underestimate the costs of their new traffic signals or their share of the overall bill for TEA-21. If so, they would reward their legislator for providing the traffic signals, even though the benefits of this project are less than the taxes they paid to fund TEA-21.

However, rational constituents may reward their legislator for his efforts to arrange pork-barrel projects even when they have a good idea of the benefits they're receiving and the cost they're paying. Why? Because it's easy to see that the proposal will be enacted regardless of whether it contains something for them. So while constituents can demand that their district not get anything from a distributive proposal, the only thing this does is ensure that they pay their share of the proposal's costs but receive nothing in return.

For example, suppose that when TEA-21 was in the planning stage, voters in Compton told their representative that they knew their share of TEA-21's costs would exceed the value of new traffic signals, so they didn't want this project or anything else included in TEA-21. Their representative would respond by having the project removed from the highway bill and would probably vote against the proposal when it came up for consideration.

Would the representative's efforts defeat the bill? No—she is only one vote of many. The only certain effect is that TEA-21 wouldn't contain anything for the citizens of Compton. In other words, by refusing their share of pork-barrel projects, voters in Compton would be cutting off their noses to spite their faces. They would be moving from a situation where they paid some costs and received some benefits, to one where they paid some costs and received no benefits.

Thus, even when rational constituents know that the projects contained in a distributive proposal have costs greater than benefits, they have a strong incentive to demand that their district receive its fair share. Knowing this preference, rational legislators favor universalism, even when this practice amounts to stuffing a distributive proposal with projects that have high costs and low benefits. The result is distributive proposals that sail through Congress and are politically popular back home, even as legislators and voters all complain about the evils of the pork barrel.

The Pork Barrel and Rationality

This section has explained why rational legislators work to deliver pork-barrel projects to their districts and why rational constituents reward this behavior. As you have seen, the pressure to "bring home the bacon" exists even when everyone knows that the projects being funded are of questionable worth. Moreover, this pressure also leads to the expansion of distributive proposals and has other damaging consequences.

These conclusions reinforce a point made in Chapter One. The fact that legislators and constituents are rational does not imply that their actions always have favorable consequences or that they always do the right thing by some objective standard.

Rationality does not ensure any of these effects. When a rational actor faces a decision, he takes whatever action he expects will lead to the best-possible outcome or set of outcomes. As shown here, these calculations can lead to outcomes no one likes, including the enactment of wasteful distributive legislation. However, the fact that these outcomes are disliked makes them no less rational.

Thus, when rational members of Congress write a distributive proposal, the strong incentive is to deliver projects to everyone—to any district that can even come close to qualifying, regardless of whether the project's costs exceed its benefits. Members of Congress do not have the incentive to kill off these wasteful projects. In fact, working to supply wasteful projects to their constituents is a good way to get reelected.

Does this description mean that every proposal Congress enacts is full of wasteful projects? No. The pressure to expand programs and use them to build political support is always there. But even in the most extreme case, a program like TEA-21, a sizable share of the

budget is used to address real national problems with projects that
would have received funding even if political factors were irrelevant.
True, the documentary on infrastructure awareness may have been a
political plum for some lucky constituent. But the traffic signals in
Compton, the bridge in Vermont, and other projects like them probably would have received congressional funding even if politics
wasn't a factor in the allocation process.

The bias introduced by credit claiming is also reduced by the use
of formulas to distribute funds. For example, nearly 90 percent of the
TEA-21 budget was given to communities on the basis of population
and other factors, while 10 percent went to pork-barrel projects.[7]
Thus, larger communities received more transportation money than
did to smaller ones.

Formula-based allocations are resistant to political manipulation—
not so much because it's hard to monkey with the formula, but because it's hard to claim credit for funds given out by formula. It's
easy to take responsibility for a project. Picture the representative
from Compton, pointing to the new traffic signals and telling constituents how she worked to make sure that this project, one of many
equally worthy ideas, made it into the final bill.

In contrast, formula money goes right into a community's budget
and is spent with all the other funds. Under these conditions, a representative can't point to an identifiable road, bridge, or some other
thing, and explain how he made it happen. As a result, credit claiming for formula-based allocations is extremely difficult.

It is also important to remember that the desire to claim credit has
effects that go well beyond funding projects of dubious merit. One
additional problem is that members of Congress will tend to ignore
issues and policy areas that offer little or no opportunities for credit
claiming. Why? Because getting involved in these areas—writing proposals, making speeches, lobbying colleagues, etc.—can do little to
help a member get reelected. Without this incentive, the temptation
is to focus attention elsewhere.

Take foreign aid. The amount of foreign aid given out by the
United States is quite low compared to other industrialized nations.
The average member of Congress knows little about the annual for-

---

[7]Does the fact that 90 percent of TEA-21 funds were distributed using formulas
mean that the share of pork barrel from this proposal wasn't all that big? Not really.
Remember that TEA-21 had a $250 billion price tag, so 10 percent of that sum is
still a large number.

eign aid bill and cares less. Moreover, the average member makes no attempt to learn about the aid programs and certainty does not waste time lobbying colleagues to vote for these proposals.

Why the lack of interest in foreign aid? Because there's nothing in the foreign-aid bill to claim credit for—most of the money gets spent outside the United States. Hence, unless a member finds foreign policy interesting or unless she comes from that rare district where constituents care about foreign aid, the member will not pay close attention to foreign-aid legislation. The results are relatively low foreign-aid budgets, with members of Congress having virtually no role in deciding how the money is spent.

Another problem with members' desire to claim credit is that the drive to write Christmas tree bills makes it hard to enact small, experimental programs. Such experiments allow government agencies to try new things—test out new solutions to problems in society. For example, one of the primary virtues of the welfare reform legislation enacted by Congress in 1996 is that it allows states to experiment with different kinds of work requirements and subsidies.

Of course, not all policy innovations work. In fact, you should expect a high failure rate. But funding some promising experiments is necessary if government is to develop better ways of dealing with problems in society.

The problem is that the drive to create opportunities for credit claiming can turn small experimental programs into large, expensive boondoggles. The classic example is a program called Model Cities, which was enacted in the late 1960s.[8] The original version of Model Cities was intended to fund between five and ten innovative projects that would try out new ways to prevent or reverse the decay of central cities. However, by the time the program was enacted, it had been transformed from a small experiment to a major effort that funded projects in over 150 cities.

Was it bad to expand Model Cities? It provided many more projects than the initial proposal and allowed many more members to claim credit for delivering a Model Cities project to their district. However, expansion didn't serve the program's original purpose, which was to test new ways to fight urban decay. It's hard to say for sure, but there probably were only five to ten good new ideas about how to go about achieving this goal. The original small program

[8]Douglas R. Arnold, *Congress and the Bureaucracy* (New Haven: Yale University Press, 1978).

would have funded all of these ideas and found out which ones worked. The expanded version wound up funding many versions of the same experiments. Thus, expanding the program was wasteful, in the sense that a smaller program would have produced the same findings (which ideas worked and which didn't) at a much lower cost.

Expanding Model Cities also ensured that the program would look like a failure, in that so much of the money was spent on unsuccessful experiments. That outcome would be no surprise if Model Cities remained a small program. However, it's hard to justify a program that funds over 150 projects as an experiment. With that much money at stake, people expect results. Thus, by expanding the program, the authors of Model Cities ensured that the program would be perceived as a failure.

A final problem with credit claiming is that expanded programs may become substitutes for actions that local governments or the private sector would have taken in any case. Intuitively, the federal government should respond to big problems, situations that the private sector or local governments cannot resolve on their own. The problem is that the pressure to create opportunities for credit claiming can turn narrowly focused distributive programs into Christmas trees.

A good example of this problem is how "emergency" spending bills in Congress, designed to help communities after a natural disaster, often balloon into catch-all bills that fund a wide range of programs. Senator Ross Feingold described one such bill in 1996:

> When the appropriations bill to provide relief for the Los Angeles earthquake was introduced in the 103rd Congress, it initially did four things: provided $7.8 billion for the Los Angeles quake, $1.2 billion for the Department of Defense peacekeeping operations; $436 million for Midwest flood relief, and $315 million more for the 1989 California earthquake.
>
> By the time the Los Angeles earthquake bill became law, it also provided $1.4 million to fight potato fungus, $2.3 million for FDA pay raises, $14.4 million for the National Park Service, $12.4 million for the Bureau of Indian Affairs, $10 million for a new Amtrak station in New York, $40 million for the space shuttle, $20 million for a fingerprint lab, $500,000 for the United States Trade Representative travel office, and $5.2 million for the Bureau of Public Debt.[9]

Feingold's speech illustrates the problem. Once members know that a spending bill is sure to be enacted, they often try to attach addi-

[9] *Congressional Record*, April 24, 1997, p. S3675.

tional spending for their districts or states. The result is that the bill is transformed from a response to urgent, unanticipated needs to a mechanism for serving the reelection needs of members of Congress.

Members of Congress and Congressional Committees: Who's in Charge?

A century ago, Woodrow Wilson, a political scientist before he went into politics and eventually became president, wrote in his doctoral dissertation that "Congress on the floor is Congress on display; Congress in committee is Congress at work."[10] This generalization still holds true today. Committees are at the heart of almost everything Congress does. Most legislation is written in committee. Committee members generally plan and manage floor debate over proposals that originated in their committee. And as Chapter Seven will discuss in detail, committee members monitor how bureaucrats implement legislation after it is enacted.

This section considers one of the more important features of the committee system in Congress: *committee deference*. That is, committee members generally have disproportionate influence over legislation that falls within their committee's jurisdiction. (The discussion here focuses on the House of Representatives, but its conclusions are applicable to the Senate as well.)

For example, when the members of a committee reports (sends) a new proposal to the full House for consideration, legislators who are not on the committee defer to the wishes and opinions of committee members. Conversely, when committee members decide against reporting a proposal, their colleagues in the full House make no protest, even if they would have liked to consider the proposal.

Suppose, for example, that the members of the House Science Committee proposed a massive increase in funding for the space program—more shuttles, trips to the moon, space colonies, you name it—arguing that these changes are necessary to keep the American frontier spirit alive. Deference implies that other House members would accept this argument and approve the proposal, even if they think there's some chance that committee members don't know what they're talking about.

The problem with deference is simple. Why would rational legisla-

[10]Woodrow Wilson, *Congressional Government* (Boston: Houghton Mifflin, 1885).

tors give up their decision-making power to a small group of colleagues? The House of Representatives, for example, is supposed to operate by majority rule. Things should happen only if a majority (50 percent + 1) of House members want them to happen, if a majority is made better off by doing something rather than nothing.

At first glance, committee deference appears to violate this intuition of majority rule. When deference occurs, a small group of committee members—much less than a majority—determines what the House does. The danger is that committee members might use deference to act in ways that they prefer but the rest of the legislature opposes. Why do House members allow their colleagues on committees this sort of discretion?

This section shows that congressional committees are organized to maximize the benefits of deference and minimize the risks. In some cases, deference reflects the fact that committees have been organized to provide information and expertise to House members. In other cases, deference reflects a trade, where members self-select onto committees that deal with matters they care about, then agree to allow colleagues on other committees to control the passage of legislation in those committees' jurisdictions, in return for the same authority.

In both cases, deference is no accident. Members of Congress defer to committee members because they want to make well-informed choices and see committee members as unbiased experts or because deference allows them extra influence over the policies they care most about. Thus, deference is not an indication that members don't care about what Congress does. Rather, it shows how members use congressional institutions to get what they want from the legislative process.

Why Deference?

This section explains why members of Congress defer to committee members. While deference is a constant across most committees, the reason why it occurs varies across two classes of committees: *low-salience committees*, which deal with programs and policies that few legislators consider interesting or important, and *high-salience committees*, which deal with issues of national importance.

Explaining Deference: What Do Committees Do? To understand committee deference, the first thing to consider is the role that committees play in legislatures such as the U.S. House of Representatives.

The primary function of congressional committees is to develop legislative proposals for consideration by the entire House. Each committee is given a jurisdiction that defines the policy areas that the committee is responsible for.[11]

The House Science Committee is a typical low-salience congressional committee. Its jurisdiction is as follows:

1. all energy research, development, and demonstration, and projects therefor, and all federally owned or operated nonmilitary energy laboratories
2. astronautical research and development, including resources, personnel, equipment, and facilities
3. civil aviation research and development
4. environmental research and development
5. marine research
6. measures relating to the commercial application of energy technology
7. National Institute of Standards and Technology, standardization of weights and measures and the metric system
8. National Aeronautics and Space Administration
9. National Space Council
10. National Science Foundation
11. National Weather Service
12. outer space, including exploration and control thereof
13. science scholarships
14. scientific research, development, and demonstration, and projects therefor

Simply put, the job of the Science Committee is to develop legislative proposals in these fourteen areas—proposals that tell NASA how to explore space or that set limits on what the National Science Foundation can fund.

A quick look at the Science Committee's jurisdiction explains a lot about committees and about deference. The first thing is that the members of the Science Committee, like members of Congress on other committees, have a lot of work to do. They have to devise an annual budget for each of the agencies and programs in their jurisdiction, deal with new policy proposals that are referred to them,

[11]A list of House committee jurisdictions for the 106th Congress can be found at http://www.house.gov/rules/comm_jurisdiction.htm

hold hearings on policy questions, and construct their own policy initiatives.

The second thing to notice is that the description of the Science Committee's jurisdiction confirms the low-salience label attached to the committee. A few members will take an interest because of their policy concerns. A legislator might be a strong supporter of manned space exploration and thus watch to see if the committee's budget proposals provide adequate funding for NASA. A few other members, such as those elected from districts that contain large aerospace contractors, will take an interest in the committee because of the potential economic impact on their constituents.

Aside from these small groups of representatives, the remaining House members and their constituents are probably not interested in what the Science Committee does. How many legislators care about NASA or the National Science Foundation or the "National Institute of Standards and Technology, standardization of weights and measures and the metric system"? Not many. How many districts contain large numbers of voters who care about these matters? Very few.

While committee jurisdictions vary in terms of substance, many look a lot like the Science Committee, in the sense that only a small minority of House members are interested in the issues that committee members deal with. These committees are thus labeled low-salience. Salience is a measure of importance—how much an individual worries about something. Committees such as House Science are low-salience in the sense that the average House member doesn't care all that much about what kinds of policies are enacted or defeated in the committee's jurisdiction.

Another example of a low-salience committee is the House Committee on Agriculture, whose jurisdiction includes, among other things, setting farm price supports and the "adulteration of seeds, insect pests, and protection of birds and animals in forest reserves." You can argue that House members and their constituents *should* care about what government does with regard to insect pests or the protection of birds and animals. But it doesn't seem a stretch to assume that they don't.

Low-Salience Committees and Deference. Low-salience committees are a perfect setting for committee deference. What occurs is a trade between the small set of legislators who want to dominate policy making within a committee's jurisdiction and the much larger set of legislators who don't much care. The legislators who care about a committee's jurisdiction will request to be assigned to the committee, a request that each party's committee on committees will be happy to approve. Once on the committee, these legislators will, within broad limits, be allowed to write whatever policies they consider appropriate. Other House members will follow the committee's lead, approving whatever choices are supported by a majority of committee members.

Why do House members defer to the members of a low-salience committee? The answer has two parts. To begin with, legislators defer to the members of a low-salience committee because they are not very interested in what the committee does. The average member of Congress is happy to let the Science Committee handle the transition to the metric system and to let the Agriculture Committee set farm price supports. She isn't very interested in these questions and knows that the vast majority of her constituents aren't interested either. Deference allows the member to focus on other issues that she considers more important.

The second reason for deference is an unspoken agreement whereby House members trade away influence over issues they don't care about in return for being allowed extra influence over the issues they consider important. For example, members of the Agriculture Committee support the Science Committee's resolution on NASA, with the expectation that the members of the Science Committee will vote for the Agriculture Committee's farm bill (or another measure) at some future date.

Why do members go along with this deference deal? The key is that they can usually get appointed to a low-salience committee that interests them. Assignments to these committees are made by *self-selection*: Only people who ask for the assignment get it; everyone who asks has their request approved sooner or later.

When low-salience committees are dominated by members who really want to set policy in the committee's jurisdiction, deference makes a lot of sense. It allows a legislator to concentrate on the policies they care about, in return for letting other people make choices on policies that the legislator doesn't care about.

Committee deference is not unconditional—the members of a low-salience committee can't do *anything* they want. The deal that creates deference to low-salience committees contains some unwritten provisions, the most important of which is that committees cannot expect deference if they propose things that are extreme or extravagant. For example, legislators on the floor would probably reject the hypothetical Science Committee request to expand massively America's manned space program. However, Science Committee members could probably get approval of a more modest yet still significant increase in funding.

High-Salience Committees and Deference. The mechanisms that facilitate deference on low-salience congressional committees will not work on high-salience committees, those that deal with issues and policies that are considered important by most House members. Examples of high-salience committees in the U.S. House include the Appropriations Committee and the Ways and Means Committee.

The difference between high-salience and low-salience committees is fundamental. Low-salience committees like House Science deal with things that few legislators care about. In contrast, most members have strong preferences about the policies that fall into high-salience jurisdictions. For example, the job of the Appropriations Committee is to write the House's version of the annual budget of the United States. Similarly, the Ways and Means Committee has jurisdiction over the tax code, Social Security, and Medicare.[12]

At first glance, high-salience committees should not receive the same kind of deference that is accorded to low-salience committees. Why? Because these committees deal with issues that everyone in the House cares about. Legislators not on these committees are unwilling to let committee members act as they think best—they want to get involved in making these choices.

However, deference is just as common for high-salience committees as it is for low-salience committees. The reason is simple: information.

Consider the Ways and Means Committee. Republican and Democratic legislators are likely to disagree about what kinds of individual tax rates are fair and appropriate. However, they can agree on the need to have good information about the consequences of setting tax rates at one level or another, including how much revenue will be raised, the impact on economic growth rates, and how much will be paid by people at different income levels.

These questions are not easy to answer. The average House member does not have the time, the background, or the staff support

---

[12]Another sign that Appropriations and Ways and Means are high-salience committees is that assignments to the committee are *exclusive*, meaning that committee members have no other committee assignment.

needed to answer them. Thus, members face a problem: How can they make good, well-informed decisions on complex policy questions?

The answer is the committee system. The members of a high-salience committee like Ways and Means are encouraged to become experts in the issues before their assignment to the committee. The typical member of a high-salience committee has some background in his committee's jurisdiction. For example, some members of Ways and Means were lawyers before their election to the House; others were doctors or held administrative positions in the health-care industry. Committee members are also given extra staff to help them understand the implications of different policy options.

Taken together, these factors give the members of high-salience committees an information advantage over other members of Congress. These committee members are experts; they know more about the range of public problems that fall into their jurisdiction, as well as the possible solutions and their pros and cons.

Making sure that committee members are experts is only part of the answer to the deference question. Even if committee members are experts, why listen to them? Suppose you're a member of the House, and your colleagues on Ways and Means tell you that a particular proposal was good for your constituents and consistent with your policy goals. You might worry that the experts on Ways and Means are misrepresenting the truth in an attempt to get you to vote for something that's good for them but not for you or for your constituents.

This problem is addressed by the strategy used to assign members to high-salience committees. Recall that low-salience assignments are made by self-selection: Members ask to be on a low-salience committee and generally get it. In contrast, when making assignments to high-salience committees, the party caucuses in the House try to ensure that their party's representatives on the committee reflect the range of interests within their caucus.

For example, when assigning members to the Ways and Means committee, the Democratic Steering and Policy Committee selects some strong supporters of a progressive tax code, some that believe in a flat tax, and others with different preferences. The goal is to assemble a committee cohort that reflects the preferences of the entire Democratic Caucus. The Republican Committee on Committees follows a similar strategy. Simply asking to be assigned to the Ways and Means Committee does not guarantee that a member will be named.

A member will be assigned only if she helps to make the committee more representative of the caucus.

When both parties make assignments to high-salience committees in this way, the result is committees that looks like the entire House, committees where virtually any member on the floor can find someone on the committee whose interests are similar if not identical to his own.

The procedures used to assign members to high-salience committees facilitate deference. In essence, they create committees of experts who can speak to different groups on the floor, supplying them with information about policy proposals. Moreover, the fact that these committees contain members with a wide range of interests means that if the committee can agree on a policy compromise, members on the floor know that the proposal is likely to serve their interests as well.

For example, suppose that the Ways and Means committee sends a tax bill to the House floor. You're Joe Average legislator. You don't know much about the tax code or about the bill. But you know that your friend Edith Tax Lawyer, who agrees with you on most issues, is a member of the committee. Therefore, before you decide what to do, you call up Edith and ask what she thinks about the tax bill.

Should you worry about whether Edith will tell the truth? No. Since she generally wants the same things you do, she has no reason to misrepresent the truth about the tax proposal. Put another way, if she likes the bill, she'll tell you; if she doesn't like it, she'll tell you that, too.

To repeat the question, why should a House member trust a committee of experts to make decisions on high-salience proposals? Because the legislator knows there is at least one committee member with similar interests and policy preferences who can be relied on to share her expertise. This trust creates deference. As long as the members of high-salience committees can agree on a compromise proposal, they will be able to convince legislators off the committee to support it—put another way, legislators on the floor will defer to their judgment.

As this example suggests, deference to high-salience committees is a reward for good behavior and careful assignments. It is as though members on the floor of the House were to say the members of high-salience committees, "Okay, you people, we've chosen you carefully, now learn about these policy matters, figure out what we ought to do, and write it out in a policy proposal. We'll do whatever you say."

However, this deference is not automatic. Legislators defer only if they believe that a committee has done its homework and if they believe that at least some committee members want the same things they do. If committee members don't spend time learning the issues, or if the committee becomes unrepresentative, deference will disappear.

An example of how committee deference can be damaged or destroyed is found in the history of the House Appropriations Committee. Members of this committee like to refer to themselves as the "guardians of the federal treasury." Prior to 1970, deference was the norm for the Appropriations Committee. With very few exceptions, committee recommendations were approved with very little discussion or dissension. In a typical year, most speeches on the floor were by committee members describing their proposal and by other members congratulating committee members for doing a good job.

Deference by House members to the Appropriations Committee meant that if you were the head of a government agency and wanted an increase in your budget, there was no reason to talk to the average member of the House or to people on the president's staff. Rather, you had to convince the members of the Appropriations Committee that the request was justified.

What happened to the Appropriations Committee? Beginning in the late 1960s, the informal rules governing assignments to this committee broke down. As fiscal conservatives retired, the Committee on Committees in both parties assigned a number of members who wanted to use their position to get additional projects and other federal monies for their districts.[13] With this change, House members could no longer be sure that the Appropriations Committee would carry out its assigned task. On the contrary, the new committee was seen as being biased toward approving budget increases, particularly if the funds were to be spent in the districts of committee members.

After these changes in the committee's composition, deference to the Appropriations Committee's spending proposals vanished. Members on the floor spoke out against them and offered a large number of amendments to the committee's proposals designed to implement their own spending priorities. Eventually much of the Appropriations

---

[13]Why didn't the Committee on Committees continue to appoint fiscal conservatives? One problem was a shortage of fiscal conservatives in the House. The second was pressures within both parties to abandon fiscal conservatism as a make-or-break criteria for a seat on Appropriations.

Committee's power to determine the size of the federal budget was given to a new committee, the Budget Committee.

The example of the Appropriations Committee illustrates that deference to high-salience committees is not automatic. Legislators on the floor of the House defer to such committees only if they are convinced that the committees are acting as they should—serving as a source of unbiased expertise and information to the House. As this perception declines, so does deference.

Committee Deference and Rationality: A Summary

This section has explained committee deference: why members of the House of Representatives allow congressional committee members to dominate the writing of policy proposals within their jurisdiction. There are two distinct reasons for deference, one that applies to low-salience committees (e.g., Science or Agriculture) and another that applies to high-salience committees (e.g., Appropriations or Ways and Means).

In both cases, these reasons imply that the committee system is a rational choice. It has been constructed in order to help members pursue their interests. Members self-select onto low-salience committees whose jurisdiction matches their interests or is relevant to their constituents. Assignments to high-salience committees are made with the goal of making the committee representative of the entire House. High-salience committees are also given extra resources to hire aides and carry out investigations.

This analysis also shows that deference is a rational choice. On low-salience committees, deference facilitates a trade across jurisdictions, where legislators can focus on jurisdictions that interest them. And on high-salience committees, deference arises from the fact that these committees are designed to be representative, so that every member of the committee can find a committee member whose judgments they can rely on.

These explanations of committee deference show why members of the House of Representatives—an institution where majorities rule— allow minorities on committees to make policy choices for the rest of the institution. Deference does not imply that legislators are abdicating their job of making laws for the rest of us. Rather, deference is a conscious, and often efficient, choice. Sometimes this choice reflects the fact that policy choices are important to only a few legislators. At other times deference is the product of members' desire to make well-informed policy choices. In both cases, deference is designed to improve on the situation where all members give equal attention to all of the decisions before the House.

These findings also suggest that committee deference is not a bad thing. By allowing committee members to dominate the policy-making process, members are not giving up something for nothing. True, deference allows a small number of legislators to make choices for the rest of the House. But for high-salience committees, deference reflects the expectation that these choices will reflect the preferences held by members off the committee. And for low-salience committees, House members are happy to let committee members decide on policy in their jurisdiction, especially since they expect a similar deference when their own committee reports a proposal. Thus, deference gives members something for something—more information on some policies and more influence over others.

Summary

This chapter has described two examples of how rational legislators operate—how they write and vote on distributive legislation and how they shape a fundamental congressional institution, the committee system, to provide information and implement trades of influence across institutions.

This chapter also provides an example of how rational actions can lead to unfavorable outcomes. In particular, constituents sometimes demand that their legislator work to get pork-barrel projects for them (or, equivalently, reward their representative for doing so), even though the benefits they receive are outweighed by their share of the costs.

While this situation may be frustrating, it does not imply that constituents are not making the right choice. As noted earlier, it's rational for citizens to demand projects, even wasteful ones—failing to do so ensures that they will pay the costs of distributive legislation and receive no benefits. You can wish that constituents faced different choices, but you cannot blame them for behaving as they do.

The discussion of committees and deference also highlights how institutions influence what happens in Congress. The members of high-salience committees provide information to legislators off the committee. Without these institutions, the rest of the House would lack the expertise needed to make well-informed choices on complex, important policy questions.

Similarly, the role of committees as a source of legislative proposals allows members to use them to facilitate an influence trade across low-salience jurisdictions. Without committees, these trades would have to be arranged on the floor of the House, a time-consuming and uncertain process.

In both cases, committees matter. These institutions change both the behavior of individual House members and the outcomes that result from their behavior. They are a clear example of the important role that institutions play in the political process—and an example of how politicians use institutions to achieve their goals.

～7～

The Separation of
Powers and the
Executive Branch

T his chapter examines a fundamental institution of America's national government: the separation of powers between the executive and legislative branches. The first part of the chapter examines how the separation of powers is affected by the president's veto power.[1] How much power does the veto give him? Does it make the president an equal partner in the legislative process? something more? something less? To answer these questions, we have to focus on the rules—when and how the president can veto legislation, how his veto can be overturned.

But the impact of rules depends on the situation. As you will see, the veto gives the president significant power over the legislative process. The amount of power, however, depends on how many

---

[1]This discussion does not consider pocket vetoes, whereby a president kills a bill by failing to act on it (sign it into law or veto it) at a time when Congress is not in session. While pocket vetoes do occur, they almost never involve legislation of any significance. If members of Congress are concerned about a pocket veto, they will remain in session until the president has dealt with their proposal. This discussion also assumes that a majority in Congress opposes whatever the president wants to do. Why? Because when there is agreement the veto doesn't come into play; the veto is valuable only when the president and Congress are at odds.

members share the president's preferences, whether the president is happy with the status quo or wants to change it, and the timing of the veto decision. In short, this section will illustrate a central theme: The rules matter. It will also illustrate the fact that the rules are not used in a vacuum.

Once legislation is enacted, it must be implemented. Implementation is the job of bureaucrats in the executive branch. This separation between writing laws and putting them into effect creates a new task for members of Congress: oversight, or determining whether bureaucratic actions are consistent with the intent of the laws they were given to implement.

Members of Congress are often accused of ignoring their oversight responsibilities. If members are rational actors and are concerned with the ultimate impact of their votes and actions, why do they seem unconcerned with implementation? Does the absence of oversight mean that bureaucrats can do whatever they want, free of congressional scrutiny?

In fact, there is a lack of formal oversight. But this exists because members use an alternate mechanism for keeping track of bureaucratic actions, a mechanism that transfers the work of scrutiny outside the legislative branch to interest groups and individuals. As a result, members of Congress can do relatively little investigating while remaining well informed about bureaucratic actions and ready to correct attempts to deviate from their instructions. In other words, the discussion of oversight provides another example of how behavior in politics that looks thoroughly irrational can, in fact, be completely optimal. This will be the focus of the second part of this chapter.

The Power of the Veto

Our federal Constitution is based on the idea of *checks and balances*—the notion that no branch of the federal government (legislative, executive, or judicial) can make policy by itself. The veto power is one of the institutions that translate this principle into concrete rules and procedures. The Constitution specifies two distinct procedures for enacting laws:

- A proposal receives a simple majority in the House and the Senate (218 votes in the House and 51 in the Senate), plus the president's consent.

THE SEPARATION OF POWERS

• A proposal receives a majority vote in Congress, a presidential veto, then passage through both houses by two-thirds (287 votes in the House and 67 in the Senate).

The president must also act within ten days, if the legislature is in session, or the bill automatically becomes law.

As an example, consider a proposal to ban late-term abortions. This proposal received majorities in the Republican-controlled House and the Senate when it was first voted on in 1997. President Clinton vetoed the measure in summer 1998. The House voted 296–132, more than enough to override. However, the override attempt in the Senate failed on a vote of 64–33.[2]

As this example illustrates, a president can sometimes use the veto to stop the legislative process in its tracks. By vetoing the late-term abortion ban, President Clinton seriously weakened the chance that the proposal would become law, despite the fact that it initially received majorities in both houses of Congress.

Of course, not all presidential vetoes are successful. For example, in December 1995, both houses of Congress overrode President Clinton's veto of a bill intended to curb frivolous lawsuits by investors against public corporations.[3] The vote was 68–30 in the Senate and 319–100 in the House.

This section considers a fundamental question about the veto: How much power does it convey to the president? Does the president usually get what he[4] wants—either from using the veto or because the threat of a veto, real or implied, forces members of Congress to accommodate the president's wishes in the first place? Or are members of Congress generally able to ignore veto threats?

If you put this question to most people, they will come back with one of two responses. The first is that the president's ability to veto legislation makes him an equal partner in the legislative process. That is, since the president can use the veto to stop members of Congress from enacting legislation and since the president cannot enact legislation by himself, members of the two branches are forced to work together to solve national problems.

---

[2]Julia Duin, "Senators Fail to Ban Abortion Procedure; Fall 3 Votes Short of Veto Override," *Washington Times*, September 19, 1998, p. A1.

[3]Aaron Zitner, "For First Time, Veto by Clinton Overridden," *Boston Globe*, December 23, 1995, p. 1.

[4]Note that I use masculine pronouns throughout to refer to "the president." That's because we have not (yet) elected a woman president.

A more sophisticated response would be that, even with the veto power, members of Congress are in the legislative driver's seat. After all, presidential vetoes are conditional in that they can be overridden. In contrast, when the president wants to do something that a majority of House members and Senators oppose, they can preserve the status quo by simply refusing to enact the necessary laws.

Along these lines, members of Congress can also be seen as having a *first-mover advantage*. That is to say, when a president considers how to respond to legislation enacted by Congress, he has a very limited choice: sign the legislation into law or veto it. The president cannot pick and choose among the provisions of a bill, signing into law the ones that he likes and vetoing the rest.[5]

The fact that a president's veto power is so limited suggests that members of Congress could pack a bill with all sorts of provisions that a president doesn't want, knowing that as long as they include some features that the president does want, he will be forced to sign it. Insofar as they can do this, the president is at a significant disadvantage when he negotiates with members of the House and Senate over the details of legislative proposals.

The next section considers the intuitions of presidential-congressional equality and congressional superiority and finds that both are wrong. A president's ability to get the policy outcomes he wants varies depending on factors such as the size of the coalition in the House and Senate that supports a particular policy initiative, whether the president is happy with policy as it stands or wants to change things, and the amount of time remaining in the legislative session. These are only some of the factors that shape presidential influence, but they are enough to show that the president's veto is indeed worth something, something that varies with the situation.

What Difference Does the Veto Make— And When Does It Make a Difference?

This section describes how the situation affects a president's ability to use the veto (or the threat of a veto) to influence the kinds of policies

---

[5]In contrast, almost all state governors have a *line-item veto*, meaning that they can veto part of a legislative proposal while accepting the remainder. The extent of the power varies across states—some governors can change one word or number, while others are limited to accepting or rejecting entire sections of a proposal. The president was granted the line-item veto for a short period, but the Supreme Court ruled it unconstitutional in 1998.

that are enacted in the House and Senate. Remember that the president can veto any legislation Congress sends him, and Congress can override his veto with the support of two-thirds of both houses. But the president must act within ten days (when Congress is in session), otherwise, the bill becomes law automatically. So the president's veto power is seriously affected by the size of the congressional coalition in favor of a piece of legislation, the president's intentions (to preserve the status quo or to do something new), and the timing of the veto (at the beginning, middle, or end of a congressional session).

Size of the Congressional Majority. As we discussed above, enacting a piece of legislation requires only a simple majority in the House and in the Senate,[6] veto overrides require a two-thirds majority.

So if the president doesn't like some proposal but knows that more than two-thirds of House members and Senators are willing to vote for it, the president's ability to veto legislation isn't going to be very useful. If he vetoes the proposal, supporters in the House and Senate will simply override the veto.

The 1995 bill to deter frivolous lawsuits was a situation in which the president's veto was rendered irrelevant. More than two-thirds of House and Senate members had voted for the lawsuit bill when it was first enacted. And support for the proposal remained firm even after President Clinton issued his veto. Thus, the only effect the veto had was to make members of Congress vote for the proposal a second time.

This example identifies by negation the kind of situation in which the president's veto matters, where it gives him some bargaining power against members of Congress. Simply put, the president's veto has power only in situations where the coalition of legislators who want to do something—make new laws or regulations, spend money, or otherwise change public policy—is large enough to command a simple majority in both Houses of Congress but *not* large enough to get a two-thirds vote. Under these conditions, the legislature needs the president's support to enact the proposal.

What kinds of legislation does the president's veto powers affect? A good example is the 1999 Republican tax cut proposal. Republicans in both houses were solidly behind the proposal. However, there were only 55 Republicans in the Senate and 223 in the House. Thus, a unified Republican party could pass their proposal through the

[6]Additional votes may be needed in the Senate to close off debate.

House and Senate but couldn't muster enough votes in either chamber to override a presidential veto and were therefore dependent on getting President Clinton's support for their proposal in order to enact it.

What Does the President Want? The second factor that affects the president's ability to bargain with members of Congress has to do with his preferences. Simply put, is the president interested in preserving the status quo, or does he want to change governmental policy?

To say that the president wants to preserve the status quo means that he is happy with what our government is doing in some policy area. For example, a president might feel that the current restrictions on abortion strike the right balance between a woman's right to choose and the government's interest in ensuring safe and ethical medical procedures. If so, the president's principal goal in this policy area is to prevent members of Congress from making any changes to the law.

The opposite situation would be one in which a president preferred a different policy to the status quo. In the case of abortion policy, for example, a president might want to end all restrictions on the procedure or favor making abortion completely illegal. These two policy goals are very different, but they share one thing in common: In both cases, the president's goals imply that he wants to change the status quo, changing abortion policy to one that is closer to his ideal.

But the president cannot himself initiate legislation—say, to narrow or widen abortion rights—so he is dependent on Congress. Simply put, what good is the president's constitutional power to veto legislation when a majority of members don't want to enact something in the first place?

A recent example of the president's inability to initiate congressional consideration of proposals is the fate of President Clinton's Social Security reforms. The president set out proposals in his 1999 State of the Union address to invest some Social Security receipts in the stock market, where they would average higher rates of return than under the current practice of using the funds to purchase government bonds. However, congressional Republicans, a majority in both the House and the Senate, were unified in their opposition to this proposal. Clinton's power to recommend legislation was of little help in getting members of Congress to vote on or even to consider these proposals.

In general, the veto power is very useful to a president who is happy with the status quo—as long as members of Congress cannot assemble a two-thirds majority in both chambers, the president can use the veto to prevent changes in government policy. In contrast, the veto power is of little help to presidents who want to change existing policies. Such changes require congressional initiative, and there is no way to use the veto to gain such consent.

In light of this discussion, let's consider two proposals that were voted on during the 106th Congress. One is the attempt to ban late-term abortions. As described earlier, this proposal received majorities in both houses of Congress, was vetoed by President Clinton, and the veto was sustained (it received the necessary two-thirds majority in the House but was three votes shy in the Senate).

Under these conditions, President Clinton was in the legislative driver's seat. Proponents of the late-term ban needed his signature to enact this proposal. Of course, President Clinton opposed the proposal and therefore had no reason to sign it. Rather, his policy preferences were best served by vetoing the proposal, which kept the status quo in place.

At the other extreme, consider the battle over paying the United State's annual dues to the United Nations.[7] Throughout the late 1990s, annual appropriations bills contained a provision that prohibited these payments unless the U.N. implemented a number of fiscal reforms. By late 1999, the amount in arrears approached one billion dollars.

President Clinton thought the status quo was a bad situation and supported the payment of dues. However, the mostly Republican majorities in both the House and Senate opposed payment—that is, they preferred the status quo.

Under these conditions, the president's veto power was of little use. The president wanted members of Congress to do something—to resume paying America's U.N. dues. Unfortunately, while the veto can sometimes be used to block congressional initiatives, there's no way to use it to force members of Congress to initiate consideration of a proposal. Republicans in Congress didn't need to enact a law to obtain their preferred outcome—the status quo, no payments, was exactly what they wanted. Short of threatening to veto other laws as

---

[7]Steve Mufson, "Albright Promises Family Planning Funds; Next U.S. Budget Will Restore Losses From U.N. Debt Compromise, Secretary Says," *Washington Post*, November 25, 1999, p. A06.

punishment for not voting on U.N. dues, there was nothing that the president could do.[8]

Ultimately, the U.N. dues were paid, but on terms dictated by congressional Republicans. The final version of the dues proposal made fiscal reform a requirement for dues payment—no reforms, no money. Moreover, none of the payments could be used to fund U.N. agencies that work to increase access to abortions in third-world countries. President Clinton opposed both of these provisions, but reluctantly accepted them in return for congressional support of the dues payment.

In sum, the veto power is essentially reactive—it enables the president to block congressional initiatives that he does not like, but it gives him no control over initiating legislation. The president can ask sympathetic legislators to sponsor a proposal that he would like to see enacted. But the proposal's fate in the House and Senate—whether it proceeds through committee consideration to floor debate and a vote—is in the hands of individual members.

The Timing of the Veto. The third factor that affects the president's ability to use the veto power to influence congressional decision making is the timing of the veto. That is, does the president face a veto decision at the end of a congressional term or at some other time? By sending a proposal to the president late in the session, members of Congress can sometimes gain a first-mover advantage, and thereby reduce the President's influence over what proposals look like.

Some background is in order. Congressional terms last for two years—for example, members of the 106th Congress were elected in November 1998, took office in January 1999, and will serve until January 2001. (Many will be reelected and thus serve in the 107th Congress, which will take office in January 2001.) Senate terms last for six years: Senators elected in November 1998 took office in January 1999 and will serve until 2005 (unless reelected). But one-third of Senators are up for reelection every two years.

The timing of a veto matters because members are busier at the end of a term than they are at the beginning or in the middle. At the end of a congressional term, all House members and one-third of the Senate are under great pressure to finish work and go home to campaign for reelection. The president (who is elected every four

---

[8]Moreover, these threats might backfire: The president might be forced to veto proposals that he actually favored or that were favored by congressional Democrats.

years) is either up for reelection as well or needs to campaign for candidates from his party.

Legislation is also a priority at the end of a term. For one thing, legislators must enact the annual federal budget—without a new budget, the government's ability to spend money expires each year on October first. In addition, any proposals that are not enacted by the end of a term (for example, a proposal that has passed through the House but has not been considered by the Senate) must start at the beginning of the legislative process in the next Congress.

In short, members of Congress don't have a lot of spare time at the end of a session. This heavy workload has implications for what members will do in response to a veto. Suppose the president vetoes a law at the end of a session, and everyone in Washington knows that there aren't enough votes to override the veto. What happens then? Earlier in the session, congressional leaders would meet with the president to negotiate over the terms of a compromise bill, one that would likely attract majority support in the House and Senate and receive the president's support as well. At the end of a term, however, there is no time for negotiation. Members are likely to ignore a vetoed piece of legislation—not because they don't want to see it enacted, but because they have too many other things to do before the term ends.[9]

These time pressures do not exist at the beginning or in the middle of a congressional term. In contrast to the frenzied pace at the end of a term, there is plenty of time to bargain over the shape of a compromise proposal. The president can make the first offer or wait for congressional leaders to initiate the process. This is not to say that a successful bargain is inevitable, simply that the time pressures that exist at the end of the term are not a factor.

In short, for proposals that are enacted at the end of a congressional term, the president and members of Congress know that a veto effectively kills a bill, at least for the current term and perhaps forever. True, a vetoed proposal can be brought up again in the next

---

[9]The only exceptions are a small set of proposals that must be enacted before members of Congress can adjourn. The most obvious examples are the thirteen appropriations bills that establish funding levels for government departments and agencies. Without signed appropriations bills (or short-term versions that are called continuing resolutions), the government cannot operate. As a result, members of Congress and the president are forced to arrive at an acceptable compromise on funding levels, regardless of how long it takes. The bad news is that the need to work out a budget compromise makes it even harder to resolve differences on other pieces of legislation.

Congress. However, there are likely reasons that it won't be. Other legislation may have a higher priority. The membership of Congress may change enough that no version of the proposal can get through the House and the Senate. Or there may be a new president.

Thus, the end of a congressional term creates a first-mover advantage for members of Congress—that is, they can send barely acceptable proposals to the president and say in effect, "Take it or leave it." The president faces a simple choice: Sign the bill and let it become law, or veto it and get nothing.

If members of Congress are well informed about the president's preferences, they will be able to devise a proposal that gives the president just enough that signing the proposal is better than killing it with a veto. Suppose, for example, that members of Congress and the president disagree on a bill to increase funding for the National Park Service. The president wants ten billion dollars in extra funding but also prefers any increase to no increase—he will take what he can get. A majority in the House and Senate favor a three-billion-dollar increase in funding, although the president's ideal of a ten-billion-dollar increase is also acceptable. The number of supporters in each chamber is large enough to enact a parks funding proposal but not large enough to override a veto, and the remaining House members and Senators oppose any funding increase.

What kind of proposal will ultimately be enacted? Were the pro-parks majorities in the House and Senate to enact a bill containing a three-billion-dollar increase during the middle of a congressional term, the president would veto the proposal, thinking, "If I veto this turkey, the supporters won't be able to override. Then we can get together and compromise on something that's closer to my ideal." And the president and supporters of increased parks funding in Congress would probably wind up splitting the difference between their respective ideals, compromising on an increase of six and a half billion dollars. The new version of the bill would then sail through the House and Senate and receive the president's signature. This compromise wouldn't be the president's ideal, but would be closer to what the president wants than the original three-billion-dollar proposal.

Moreover, if supporters anticipate that they will ultimately have to split the difference with the president anyway, they may decide to enact the compromise increase to start with, assuming the president would then sign the bill, ending the process without a veto and subsequent negotiation. Even so, the threat of the veto clearly changes how the bill is written.

The situation is quite different at the end of the congressional term. Now there is no time for post-veto bargaining—a vetoed proposal is dead, at least until the next congressional term. These conditions give congressional supporters of parks funding a chance to enact their ideal bill—a three-billion-dollar increase—and say to the president, "If you veto this proposal, the result will be no funding increase at all, since it's too late in the term to work out a compromise. Go ahead, make our day."

How will the president respond? He wants a larger increase than what members of Congress are offering but he knows that it's late in the session and that a veto kills any chance for increasing parks funding. Thus, since the president prefers the congressional proposal to the status quo, his best choice is to sign the bill.

This example shows how the importance of the president's veto power depends on the situation—here, on whether there is time to negotiate after a veto is issued. When there is time for bargaining and compromise, the president can use the veto (or threaten to do so) to move congressional proposals closer to his ideal. But at the end of a term, when a veto effectively kills a proposal, the veto is much less useful. As long as members of Congress are careful to enact something that the president likes even a little more than the status quo, the president will have a strong incentive to sign it, even if the proposal is far from ideal.

The Veto and Strategic Behavior

This section began by describing two intuitions about the president's veto power: one, that the executive and legislative branches were roughly equal partners in the legislative process; and, two, that members of Congress were at an advantage in that the structure of the legislative process allowed them to initiate legislation (or not), giving them the advantage of controlling what the legislation includes.

The discussion has shown that both of these intuitions are wrong. Their principal defect is the implicit assumption that the impact of the veto on the legislative process is the same across all situations. In fact, the power conveyed by the veto varies with the context. Sometimes the ability to veto legislation gives the president a lot of influence over what members of Congress do, and sometimes it gives him little or no influence at all.

For one thing, the president's ability to influence members of Congress depends on the level of congressional support he can gain. When majorities in one or both houses of Congress oppose the president's plans and refuse to initiate the legislation the president has proposed, or when a strong majority (greater than two-thirds) in both Houses wants to pass legislation, the veto doesn't help a president get what he wants. In these situations, members of Congress are driving the legislative train, and the president is left standing on the platform. He can threaten to veto legislation that passes through Congress, but this threat will not compel members to act when they don't want to or deter the passage of legislation that has a strong majority behind it.

When members of Congress cannot assemble the votes needed to override a presidential veto, you might think that the president's power is roughly equal to that held collectively by members of Congress, in that neither branch can enact legislation without the other's consent. However, the analysis here shows that this new intuition is wrong as well. The veto is fundamentally a blocking power—a way for the president to prevent members of Congress from doing something. It is of little use in persuading members of Congress to act when they are not inclined to do so.

Finally, the president's influence over the legislative process also depends on timing. When there is no time for compromise and bargaining following a veto, members of Congress have a first-mover advantage, which they can use to force the president to sign proposals that are far from his ideal—and far from what the president could have obtained earlier in the session.

These findings illustrate this book's message about the role of institutions in American politics. Simply put, the veto matters—at least some of the time—because it allows the president to influence the kinds of proposals that are enacted by members of Congress. Alternately, the president's ability to veto legislation often forces members of Congress to consider the president's preferences when they write and vote on legislation. At least some of the time, legislative outcomes are different because of the president's veto power.

In short, the veto neither makes the president into a dictator, nor ensures that he is an equal partner with Congress in the writing and enacting of legislative proposals. Rather, the impact of the veto depends on the situation. At least some of the time (e.g., when strong majorities exist in both Houses of Congress or at the end of a session), the ability to veto legislation doesn't give the president much bargaining power. At other times (e.g., when congressional majoriu~ are small and the president favors the status quo), the veto allows the president to preserve his preferred outcomes against requests for change by members of Congress.

Understanding Congressional Oversight: Police Patrols and Fire Alarms

This section considers congressional *oversight*: whether and how members of Congress keep track of what bureaucrats are doing. Oversight occurs when members try to determine whether the lofty goals expressed in a piece of legislation have actually been implemented. In essence, members engaged in oversight ask, "Are bureaucrats doing what we told them to do? And if not, why not?"

The discussion of oversight will center on an apparent paradox: While oversight would seem to be an important task for members of Congress and while many legislators stress the need for frequent, extensive investigations of the bureaucracy, relatively little direct congressional oversight actually takes place. The average member of Congress knows very little about how programs are being implemented—even programs that fall under her committee's jurisdiction. And congressional committees devote relatively modest resources (e.g., hearings or staff) to investigating the bureaucracy.

Lax congressional oversight is disturbing for three reasons. First, when oversight is lax, power flows from the legislative branch to the executive. If members of Congress are unable or unwilling to find out what bureaucrats are doing, the executive-branch bureaucrats are free to implement their personal policy goals or those of the president, regardless of what the legislation says they should do. In the extreme, this sort of freedom can undermine or even destroy constitutional checks and balances.

Lack of oversight may also encourage collusion between members of congressional committees and bureaucrats whose agencies fall under the committees' jurisdictions. Bureaucrats may ignore the stated goals of legislation and instead implement policies that are closer to the interests of the committee members who prepare their agencies' annual budget. These *iron triangles* (with organized interests being the third actor) can exist only when Congress is unconcerned about whether bureaucrats are doing what they were told.

Finally, the claim that members of Congress ignore oversight is worrisome because it conflicts with the expectation that members of Congress are rational actors. It is hard to square the notion that members are rational with this picture of indifference to the ultimate product of legislative action.

This section shows that these concerns about congressional oversight are based on a narrow, inaccurate conception of what oversight is.[10] In particular, these concerns result from understanding "oversight" as the systematic investigation of government programs by legislators and their staffs. However, systematic investigation by Congress is not the only way to monitor bureaucrats; bureaucrats can also be monitored by transferring this responsibility to people outside government.

As you will see, such alternate mechanisms for oversight allow members of Congress to focus their attention on remedying apparent violations of legislative intent, rather than searching for violations, as well as in maximizing the political benefits generated by oversight. Put another way, these mechanisms allow members of Congress to make a very rational trade: receive all the benefits that accrue from monitoring bureaucrats while saving much of the cost associated with formal investigations.

What Is Oversight?

At the most basic level, oversight involves comparing intent to implementation—checking whether bureaucrats have done what they were told to do. Oversight is necessary because acts of legislation do not implement themselves. Implementation is the job of the bureaucracy.

Bureaucrats are supposed to study the provisions of a law and then make the necessary changes in government policy and actions. Sometimes implementation is easy: The policy change mandated by a law is simple, obvious, and straightforward. For example, a resolution might instruct the Department of the Interior to double the fees it charges for allowing sheep to graze on federal lands. More commonly, though, laws are difficult to interpret; they set out broad, vague goals and leave it to the bureaucracy to figure out how to achieve these ends. For example, instead of simply being told to raise

[10]The arguments developed in this section are drawn from Mathew McCubbins and Thomas Schwartz, "Congressional Oversight Overlooked: Police Patrols versus Fire Alarms," *American Journal of Political Science* 28: 165–79.

rates, Interior might be instructed to develop and implement a new fee schedule that balances the needs of ranchers against the goal of preserving the environment.

The second type of scenario is more common than most people think and for good reason. The problem is not that members of Congress are too lazy to specify exactly what they want bureaucrats to do. Rather, it is easy to imagine situations in which bureaucrats are better informed than members of Congress about how a given outcome might be achieved. They might have experts on staff who know, for example, how much grazing can occur without significantly damaging the environment, as well as how much grazing will occur given different fee increases. Another reason to hand over this power is efficiency: If Congress had to specify all the provisions of a bill, there would be little time left for enacting new legislation.

Under these conditions, *delegation* is rational. By setting out goals but leaving means unspecified, members of Congress can tap agency expertise, while preserving their own time for all the rest of congressional business.

But leaving implementation up to bureaucrats creates two problems. First, there is the simple question of whether the bureaucrats got it right—did they do what a congressional majority wanted done? Particularly when a law specifies goals but not means, it would be easy to misinterpret a law's provisions.

Second, there is the question of whether the bureaucrats are implementing congressional goals or their own. Bureaucrats generally have their own policy preferences. When bureaucrats prefer a different outcome than the one that members of Congress had in mind, the temptation would be to substitute their own policy preferences for congressional intent.

A similar problem can arise when the president disagrees with the policy preferences held by a congressional majority. Suppose Congress passes a law by overriding a presidential veto. An unscrupulous president might pressure bureaucrats to ignore the actual intent of the law and instead implement policies that reflect the president's ideas about what should be done.

This problem of bureaucratic shirking is not an abstract one. For example, in the late 1970s, Congress enacted a law creating Superfund, a government program intended to fund the cleanup of toxic wastes in landfills, abandoned factories, and other areas. An office was created within the Environmental Protection Agency to administer the program. These bureaucrats were given the job of reviewing cleanup requests from local communities and deciding which ones to fund each year. The Superfund law established a set of general guidelines for choosing among applications based on the severity of the problem, the cost of cleanup, and so forth.

What happened? In the early 1980s, senior bureaucrats within the Superfund program, mostly appointed by President Reagan, apparently decided to ignore the criteria set out in the law for deciding which requests to fund. Instead, they concentrated superfund monies on sites in congressional districts represented by Republican legislators. Thus, instead of cleaning up the most seriously polluted sites, the Superfund law was being used to help Republican members of Congress claim credit and thereby get reelected.

The implementation of Superfund is an extreme example of a general problem. Because of honest mistakes or deliberate noncompliance, implementation is not automatic. Members of Congress must develop mechanisms for checking whether bureaucrats are doing what they were instructed to do—whether bureaucratic actions correspond to congressional intent. The question is, do members of Congress carry out this responsibility? And if they do, what mechanism do they use for performing this oversight?

How Much Oversight?

Do members of Congress really ignore their oversight responsibilities? At one level, the answer is surely no. Under current House rules, each standing committee must develop an annual oversight plan that details the policies and programs the committee plans to investigate in the next year. Many hearings are held at which committee members question agency staff. And committees issue stacks of press releases highlighting their oversight activities.

But all of this action masks a deeper truth: In the main, members of Congress devote a relatively small fraction of their time and energy to overseeing the bureaucracy. A good example can be drawn from the work of the House Science Committee. The committee's jurisdiction was discussed in the last chapter: science policy generally, ranging from energy research to the space program to the transition to the metric system.

At first glance, this committee appears to be a counterexample to the claim that members of Congress ignore oversight. In fact, the committee's current chair, James Sensenbrenner, was given an "Excellence in Programmatic Oversight Award" in 1998 by House Republicans.[11] Sensenbrenner was the only committee chair to receive such an award.

By the end of the 105th Congress (1997–1998) as noted in a Science Committee press release announcing Sensenbrenner's award:

> The Science Committee will have held 136 oversight hearings on a wide array of issues and concerns to American taxpayers. In total, the Committee has spearheaded 19 (not including works in progress) investigative reports from the General Accounting Office (GAO).[12] GAO staffers have testified before the Committee on 15 different occasions.

A second committee press release provides a list of its oversight activities during the 1997–1998 session:[13]

- Analysis of the science behind the Kyoto Global Climate Treaty and the economic harm it could pose to businesses;
- Examination of Air Quality standards at EPA to ensure sound science was used to establish the regulatory framework for ozone and air quality strategies;
- Inquiries [concerning] the Russian *Mir* space station safety standards to ensure safety of U.S. astronauts on board;
- Investigation of national security and economic implications of alleged satellite technology transfers from Loral and Hughes to the Chinese;
- Directed the Administration and encouraged the private sector to address the Y2K problem;
- Revealed management problems at Brookhaven National Lab resulting in changes that have made the lab safer to the surrounding community;
- Conducted the National Science Policy Study to examine the role of R&D in a post–Cold War world.

These press releases suggest a committee highly concerned with its oversight responsibilities. But a deeper look at the Science Committee paints a different picture of congressional oversight. Over a two-year period, committee members may have held 136 oversight

---

[11]"Sensenbrenner Earns Top Oversight Award," Press Release, House Committee on Science, October 2, 1998.
[12]The General Accounting Office is an investigative agency within Congress.
[13]"Science Committee Accomplishes More with Less During 105th Congress," Press Release, House Committee on Science, November 6, 1998.

hearings to cover their jurisdiction, but some of these hearings appear to have had more to do with publicity than investigation. For example, the only output from an October 6, 1998, hearing on Russia's contribution to the International Space Station was a statement by Representative Sensenbrenner about the failure of NASA's negotiations with the Russians.[14]

A better measure of oversight would be to count the number of investigations conducted by committee staff or by GAO staff. One press release lists seven investigations; the other refers to nineteen investigations conducted by the GAO at the committee's request. Some of these studies appear to be full-blown inquiries into what an agency is doing, while others (". . . encouraged the private sector to address the Y2K problem") appear to have more to do with getting committee members some media attention.

Suppose you concede that all of the Science Committee's hearings were focused on oversight rather than on developing new proposals or attracting publicity. Suppose you assume that all of the investigations listed above were detailed examinations of agency policies and actions. Even then, it appears that in any given year, many of the agencies and programs that fall under the committee's jurisdiction will receive little or no oversight. One hundred thirty-six hearings and nineteen investigations is not a lot, given that the committee's jurisdiction includes energy research and development, astronautical research and development, civil aviation research and development, environmental research and development, marine research, commercial application of energy technology, the National Institute of Standards and Technology, the National Aeronautics and Space Administration, the National Space Council, National Science Foundation, National Weather Service, outer space, science scholarships, and other programs and agencies. Each of these agencies administers numerous programs and other governmental functions. The total number is uncertain, but it is surely quite high.

In sum, even if you believe that congressional oversight statistics imply a strong commitment to oversight, the number of hearings and investigations that are undertaken in a given year are much smaller than the number of agencies and programs that are worthy of investigation. Thus our question here: Do rational legislators really ignore their oversight responsibilities, and if so, why?

---

[14]"Sensenbrenner Rebukes Administration for Space Station Failures," Press Release, House Committee on Science, October 6, 1998.

Oversight as Police Patrol

The case of Representative Sensenbrenner and the Science Committee captures the intuitive picture of congressional oversight as a kind of police patrol. Committee members who followed the *police-patrol oversight model* would begin each year by selecting a number of agencies within their jurisdiction to investigate. Throughout the year, they and their staff would undertake a thorough comparison of agency actions with the appropriate congressional mandates. After much study, they would recommend appropriate changes and sanctions to ensure that these agencies behaved as they were supposed to.

The current rules of the House of Representatives encourage police-patrol oversight. At the beginning of every session of Congress, each standing committee must file an oversight plan that sets out the programs and topics that will be investigated over the next two years.

However, the discussion of the Science Committee's oversight activities highlights four critical problems with the police-patrol model. The first problem has already been identified: coverage. Representative Sensenbrenner's award suggests that the Science Committee is one of the better House committees in terms of the quantity and quality of its oversight. Even so, there is no doubt that many of the agencies that fall within the committee's jurisdiction will receive little or no attention in any given year. If police-patrol oversight is the only way that members of Congress can watch over the bureaucracy, then it appears that bureaucrats are largely on their own, operating free of congressional scrutiny.

The second problem with police-patrol oversight is efficiency. Most of the time, congressional investigators will undoubtedly find that bureaucrats are doing more or less what they are supposed to do. Why? In general, most bureaucrats gravitate to jobs where they have no reason to violate congressional intent—either because they have no strong feelings one way or the other or because they agree with what Congress tells them to do. Rogue programs such as Superfund are likely to be the exception rather than the rule. So if examining every program or agency in rotation is required, committee members will be spending a great deal of time and turning up very few problems.

The way to increase the efficiency of police-patrol oversight is to identify the kinds of programs where violations are likely. No doubt members of congressional committees try to make this calculation when they devise their oversight plans. But without actually doing some investigation, it may be difficult or even impossible for members to determine where their oversight resources should be focused.

The third problem with police-patrol oversight has to do with its threat value. If committee members can only investigate a few of the agencies and programs within their jurisdiction in any given year, then the threat of being investigated is not going to have much impact. From the viewpoint of a would-be rogue bureaucrat, by the time Congress gets around to investigating the bureaucrat's agency, the damage will have been done—the contract will have been set, the concrete will have been poured, and the new program will be in place. The bureaucrat may even be in an entirely different job, perhaps even outside government and beyond congressional sanction.

A final problem with police-patrol oversight has to do with incentives: Will members of Congress and their staffs actually be motivated to carry out thorough investigations? The answer is, maybe not. Committees must prepare and submit an oversight plan, but having a plan does not ensure that it will be carried out or carried out well. Oversight takes time and resources. It is fundamentally detail work: poring over budgets, contracts, and memoranda; doing site visits in obscure, drab places; and preparing for hearings that few people will notice or be interested in. And some sizable fraction of the time, members will conclude that an agency is behaving more or less according to plan. It is hard to imagine an activity that has a smaller payoff in terms of reelection, policy, or any of the other goals that members typically hold.

In sum, if you think of oversight in terms of the police-patrol model, it is hard to see how rational members of Congress can exercise systematic control over the bureaucracy. Perhaps members can focus on a small number of programs they consider important; perhaps they can devise mandates that are clear and unambiguous; perhaps they can take a greater role in selecting the bureaucrats who will direct implementation. Even so, if police-patrol oversight is the primary mechanism that members use to control the bureaucracy, then it looks like the average bureaucrat acts as a free agent, essentially immune from congressional scrutiny or sanction.

An Alternative to Police Patrols: Fire Alarms

So shall we conclude that bureaucrats are free agents? This would be premature because police-patrol oversight is not the only method of

congressional control. This section explores one of the most important alternative models: *fire-alarm oversight*.

The essence of fire-alarm oversight is that members of Congress
wait for people outside government to report on how agencies are
doing. These reports can come from constituents, interest groups, or
others who have an interest in an agency's actions. If the reports indicate that agencies are behaving according to legislative intent, no
further action is necessary. A report that an agency's actions contradict congressional intent will trigger additional investigation by
members and their staff, resulting in corrections or sanctions as appropriate.

Fire-alarm oversight embodies a kind of police patrol, in that
members are interested in what bureaucrats are doing and are prepared to investigate if necessary. The difference is that, with fire-
alarm oversight, members rely on people outside Congress to tell
them where to focus their attention. There is no sampling and minimal advance planning. At most, committee members develop an
oversight plan but are ready to respond to any complaints they receive.

The expectation that fire alarms are an important oversight mechanism is consistent with a series of laws that force agencies to divulge
information to people outside government. For example, before
putting a new regulation into effect, agencies are required to publish
their proposal in the weekly *Federal Register* and invite comments
from whoever is interested.

Do agency staff read these comments? Maybe yes, maybe no.
What's more important about this *notice-and-comment procedure* is
that it forces agencies to reveal their intentions before any change in
policy actually occurs. People outside the agency can then scrutinize
the new rules and regulations, and notify members of Congress if
they see something that runs counter to what the agency has been
told to do.

A second informational mechanism that helps outsiders to learn
what an agency is doing is the Freedom of Information Act or FOIA.
This act established a procedure whereby citizens can force an agency
to release internal documents and memos—even Post-It notes. Here
again, FOIA allows people outside government to function as information sources for members of Congress and their staffs.

Example of a Fire Alarm: NASA Watch. Suppose you are a member of the House Science Committee, assigned to the Space and

Aeronautics Subcommittee. You have a number of agencies to monitor, including the National Aeronautics and Space Administration (NASA). Where do you get your information?

One possibility is an Internet site, NASA Watch.[15] NASA Watch is run by Keith Cowling, a onetime NASA bureaucrat, now a private contractor and webmaster. His site, updated several times a day, provides detailed information on the status of various NASA programs, including the international space station, the space shuttle, and various unmanned projects.

What makes Cowling's site particularly useful for our hypothetical staffer is the vast number of internal NASA documents and other confidential information that appears daily, plus detailed analysis. Over the last few years, Cowling has released various confidential memos ("Office of Space Flight Top Ten Problems, October 15, 1998"), the minutes of meetings among senior NASA staff, as well as an anonymous engineer's weekly progress reports on space station construction.

Some of the documents on Cowling's site describe situations that NASA managers would no doubt prefer to keep quiet. For example, the September 7, 1997, "Space Station This Week" report noted that:

> Building 4708 @ MSFC [Marshall Space Flight Center] had its power cut during the Labor Day weekend. The LAB, HAB, Airlock, MDMs, cables, racks, etc., [all vital station hardware] were exposed to 95-degree temperatures and 100% humidity. It is still not known if any damage was done to the flight equipment and support stuff.

In short, Cowling's site provides information on how things are really going inside NASA, rather than how people in the agency would like things to appear. In the case of the station hardware over Labor Day weekend, Cowling's report suggests that someone at NASA is not doing a good job of protecting fragile mechanisms from extreme temperatures and humidity.

A second example of the kind of information that NASA Watch provides to readers is its analysis of the *Triana* program. *Triana* is a satellite designed to provide real-time pictures of Earth that can be downloaded from the Internet. The idea was suggested by Vice Pres-

[15]www.reston.com/nasa/watch.html

ident Albert Gore and immediately became a priority project within NASA.

Suppose our Science Committee staff person wants to learn more about *Triana*. Will the satellite provide new and interesting information? Is the program being run according to established procedures and policies? These questions could be answered by an extensive investigation of the *Triana* Program Office within NASA. A far easier tactic would be to monitor the NASA Watch website, where *Triana* is referred to as "GoreSat."[16]

A few months after work started on *Triana*, Cowling showed that the pictures it is designed to take could be obtained from weather satellites that are already in orbit. He later published an E-mail from "someone@nasa.gov" that highlighted additional problems:[17]

> Another note on GoreSat: It's currently manifested for STS-107, which is pretty much the only orbital research opportunity (other than AXAF delivery and SRTM) between Neurolab (4/98) and the beginning of useful ISS ops in '02 ('01 if we're lucky). The microgravity community has lots of stuff we'd like to fly on 107, and we're willing to stretch our Russian-bled budgets to do so, but . . . damn . . . turns out there's a weight limitation due to some heavy baggage in the cargo bay.

After some consultation with Cowling, this E-mail can be translated as follows. NASA claims that *Triana* can ride for free on the space shuttle—it won't displace any other cargo. This E-mail paints a different picture. It reveals that NASA plans to fly *Triana* on the only shuttle mission in the next few years that's dedicated to research. Moreover, the weight of the *Triana* satellite has grown to the point that the only way to include *Triana* on this mission is to offload a number of microgravity experiments from the shuttle's cargo bay. In other words, the author of the E-mail is charging that NASA's internal plans for *Triana* don't match its public statements.

Information sources like NASA Watch function as fire alarms for members of Congress. Rather than undertaking a systematic investigation of NASA, committee members and staff can rely on NASA

---

[16]See http://www.reston.com/nasa/goresat.html

[17]This E-mail is not unique. As Richard Kolker, the operator of a similar website, once put it, "Anyone who thinks NASA or its contractors can keep a secret doesn't read NASA Watch." See http://www.space-frontier.org/cgi-bin/bbs/spacepolicy/read/spacepolicy/806.

Watch and its anonymous contributors to tell them which programs are worthy of committee attention. In effect, NASA Watch tells committee staff what questions to ask and provides an independent source by which to verify NASA's responses.

Do members of the Science Committee and their staff really read NASA Watch? Several pieces of information suggest they do. One is that Cowling has been invited by the committee to deliver testimony on various matters. A second comes from Cowling's server logs, which record the identity of computers that have been used to visit the NASA Watch site. As he notes,

> For what it is worth, our web server logs over the past several years clearly show that a number of specific individuals in Congress, the White House (and its offices), NASA Public Affairs, the Administrator's office, and a number of Associate Administrators and Center Director's offices regularly visit NASA Watch.[18]

NASA Watch has also been cited by members during hearings. For example, during hearings in fall 1999 on space-shuttle safety, Representative Dana Rohrabacher, chairman of the Subcommittee on Space and Aeronautics, noted that he and his staff had first learned about the shuttle's problem with frayed electrical wiring by reading NASA Watch.[19]

Finally, the best evidence of NASA Watch's role as a fire alarm is that after Cowling was twice denied press credentials by NASA the chairman of the House Science Committee, James Sensenbrenner, wrote NASA's associate administrator a letter asking for the basis for this decision.[20] Clearly, the members of the committee favor giving Cowling as much access to NASA as possible, because the information Cowling receives will soon be in their hands.

NASA Watch is only one example of an organization that provides a fire alarm to Congress. Many interest groups and think tanks can provide this sort of information by doing research on their own, preparing testimony and supporting information for a committee

---

[18]www.reston.com/nasa/internet.html, entry for April 21, 1998.
[19]Hearings on Space Shuttle Safety, Subcommittee on Space and Aeronautics, September 23, 1999.
[20]Letter from Representative Sensenbrenner to Peggy Wilhide, Associate Administrator for Public Affairs, dated July 28, 1999, and posted on NASA Watch. As of November 1999, NASA has agreed to reconsider its criteria for distribution of press credentials, so Cowling may get his credentials after all.

hearing, obtaining and releasing internal agency memos, or simply by calling committee staff and letting them know about what an agency is doing.

Why provide information? Serving as Congress's fire alarm allows these individuals to have an indirect but significant influence on the policy process. Cowling, for example, apparently believes in NASA's mission of exploring space, but thinks that agency staff care too much about doing the politically popular thing (e.g., *Triana*) and not enough about doing good science. Keeping the Science Committee well informed about NASA's misdeeds and occasional successes is Cowling's strategy for trying to change how the agency operates.

The Advantages of Fire Alarms. As we noted above, the police-patrol model has four problems: coverage, efficiency, lack of threat value, and lack of incentives for members of Congress. The fire-alarm model avoids these problems.

Fire-alarm oversight avoids the problem with coverage by removing the need to make a systematic comparison of agency mandates and agency actions. Members of Congress can't investigate regularly even a large fraction of the programs they're charged with overseeing. But with the fire-alarm model, they don't need to. They can simply wait for a violation to be reported and then focus on confirming that something has gone wrong and devising an appropriate remedy. Alternately, members can plan a systematic investigation of a small set of programs that they consider important or politically salient, allowing outsiders to monitor the rest of their jurisdiction. Narrowing the scope of oversight also makes the fire-alarm model more efficient. Under the police-patrol model, members of Congress and their staffs must spend considerable time and resources searching for deviations from congressional intent. Some fraction of the time, this search will have no obvious benefit, as the investigation will find that the agency is behaving more or less as instructed.

Narrowing the scope of oversight not only saves members' time, it also minimizes the expense of monitoring. Rather than spending time and resources keeping track of what the bureaucracy is doing, members of Congress allow people and organizations outside the institution to incur these monitoring costs. NASA Watch, for example, doesn't receive a subsidy from the Science Committee to cover the cost of running the site or its efforts to investigate NASA's policy choices. Under a police-patrol model of oversight, the committee's members and staff would incur these costs. By using NASA Watch as a fire alarm, committee members get all the benefits of Cowling's information without having to pay for it.

Fire-alarm oversight also makes a greater threat to bureaucrats who might consider ignoring what a congressional majority tells them to do. Since the police-patrol model means that the likelihood of an investigation is small, even if the penalty for violating a congressional mandate is high, this threat will not have much influence on the bureaucrat's actions, simply because the likelihood that she will face the penalty is very small. The situation changes when members of Congress are primed to respond to fire alarms. Now our would-be rogue bureaucrat doesn't just have to worry about a single committee. Instead, he faces the scrutiny of individuals and organizations outside Congress who may be monitoring his choices and are ready to report any violations to the appropriate committee. Because more people are watching, the odds of a deviation being discovered are much higher for the fire-alarm approach than for the police-patrol approach. Thus, if fire-alarm oversight works as advertised, the result is a more compliant, better-controlled bureaucracy.

As for offering incentives to members of Congress, the fire-alarm model allows members maximum oversight with minimal effort and allows members to focus on violations they can exploit for the greatest policy (and electoral) benefits.

Oversight and Rationality: A Summary

Congressional oversight is more about fire alarms than police patrols. The central implication is that there is more oversight going on than appears at first glance. Paradoxically, the fact that members of Congress do not perform systematic investigations of the bureaucracy is consistent with both abdication and high levels of control. The notion that control requires investigation ignores the possibility that members of Congress allow people outside government to do their investigating for them.

In this way, members of Congress can do very little formal oversight (measured in absolute terms or in terms of the number of agencies and programs under their control) yet have a good understanding of what bureaucrats are doing and considerable influence over their choices. Seen in this way, the lack of formal investigation is perfectly rational.

In sum, complaints about the lack of congressional oversight appear to result from an excessively narrow definition of what oversight is and how it is performed. Oversight need not involve extensive, systematic policing of government agencies. Rather, members of Congress, even those who care deeply about the implementation of public policies can rely on people outside government to highlight situations where bureaucrats are not acting as they should. This strategy reduces the cost in time and money of performing oversight, allowing members to focus on what's most important to them—getting reelected and influencing policy.

Summary

The analysis of presidential vetoes and congressional oversight highlights central themes of this book. The assumption of rationality plays a central role in both analyses. In the case of oversight, for example, the decision to forgo extensive investigations of the bureaucracy makes sense in light of legislators' interest in conserving scarce time and resources, and the availability of information from sources outside Congress. Similarly, the success of "take it or leave it" legislation is easily explained only if you assume that the president is a rational actor who will sign these proposals even if he knows that members of Congress are exploiting their institutional advantage.

Institutions play an important role in the explanations of the effectiveness of the veto and congressional oversight, too. The analysis of the veto shows how factors such as the size of congressional majorities and the timing of veto decisions can affect the president's bargaining power. And the analysis of congressional oversight shows that institutions established by the Administrative Procedures Act and the Freedom of Information Act play a critical role in facilitating fire-alarm oversight.

— 8 —

Strategy on the Supreme Court

The primary function of the Supreme Court is judicial review. By a simple majority vote, the nine members of the Court can strike down (render null and void) laws, treaties, executive orders, agency rulings, and other governmental actions that justices find to be inconsistent with some provision of the Constitution. These decisions resolve specific cases, but they also set precedent—the rules and limitations embodied in the Court's decisions are binding on similar cases in the future.

In making their decisions, the members of the Supreme Court are literally supreme. People who don't get what they want from the Court have no further recourse except to try to convince members of Congress to pass new legislation that will pass constitutional muster or to lobby Congress and state legislatures to amend the Constitution. As one chief justice once wrote, "from this Court there is no appeal."

Following the central themes of this book, the first part of this chapter describes an example of rational action on the Supreme Court, while the second shows how institutions embedded in the U.S. Constitution limit the power of judicial review.

In particular, the first section focuses on how the method of voting on Supreme Court decisions creates opportunities for strategic behavior. This method allows the chief justice to vote last, allowing her to side with the majority and thereby control the writing of opinions. The second section shows that the Court's judicial review power is limited by the reality of what happens after a law is held to be unconstitutional.

Both sections in this chapter assume that justices on the Court are calculating, strategic individuals, who are motivated by policy concerns. This description is a departure from what most people think about the Supreme Court. Many people think of the Court as somehow being above politics, with justices making decisions based on objective criteria ("what's right") rather than personal preferences.

What does it mean to say that justices are rational actors with policy preferences? The point is not that they are only concerned with their personal well being or that they ignore the impact their decisions have on other people. What rationality means is that each justice has an interpretation of what the Constitution says and some ideas of what government should be doing, and that their decisions on the Court reflect these interpretations and ideas. They can be motivated by a desire to do what's best for the country, driven by the goal of imposing a particular ideological vision on the rest of us, or anything in between. Either way, Supreme Court justices are rational actors. This chapter focuses on how they go about getting what they want and how institutions constrain their actions.

The Value of Voting Last

What is the value of being indecisive—of voting one way, then switching to the other? Intuitively, if you know what you want, you should make up your mind, vote, and move on.

However, in at least one well-documented case, it appears that a justice engaged in vote switching on numerous occasions. The justice in question was Warren Burger, Chief Justice of the United States, 1969–1986.[1] This section explains why Burger followed this strategy, showing that it was an extremely clever example of rational behavior—actions taken with the goal of maximizing Burger's influence over the Court's decisions.

---

[1]The Constitution refers to the presiding member of the Supreme Court as the Chief Justice of the United States, not as the Chief Justice of the Supreme Court, although this is the commonly used title.

Burger's strategy was well known to his fellow justices and other people who worked at the Court. Consider three anecdotes taken from *The Brethren*, a study of the Court during the first years of Burger's tenure as chief justice.[2] The first concerns a meeting between Burger and one of his clerks. At one point in the meeting, Burger noted that he had been in the majority on a particular case.

> The law clerk working with Burger was puzzled. Burger was in the minority on that one, the clerk reminded him. . . . Burger checked his vote book. No, he was not in the minority, he replied.
> "But before going to conference you said you would not vote that way," the clerk said.
> "I never said such a thing," Burger said crisply.

Later in the meeting, a second case was discussed. Again Burger claimed to have voted with the majority. His clerk protested:

> Excuse me, Chief, the clerk interrupted once again. How could he have been in the majority for a reversal of that conviction? This time the clerk was certain. The Chief had given his clerks a briefing after the conference and said he was for upholding.
> "That was a tentative vote," Burger replied firmly.

After the meeting, the clerk went to one of Burger's other clerks, explained the situation, and asked, "If he comes back and denies it [switching votes], I want you to know that he said he would do it. And when he denies it, I want you to tell me that I'm not losing my memory." (p. 66)

Burger's colleagues also noted his tendency to switch his votes. Justice William Brennan referred to Burger's votes during conference as "phony votes," because he believed that Burger would alter his vote if necessary to stay on the majority side (p. 418). A second justice, Harry Blackmun, complained that Burger would not commit himself on a case until he was sure which side had a majority (p. 174). And a third justice, William O. Douglas, believed that Burger switched his votes on a series of abortion cases decided in early 1970s as a way of manipulating the outcome (p. 171).

Why was Burger so interested in being on the winning side? As you will see, Burger didn't act this way because he was indecisive or be-

[2]Bob Woodward and Scott Armstrong, *The Brethren: Inside the Supreme Court*, (New York: Simon and Schuster, 1979).

cause he liked being on the winning side. Rather, the strategy maximized Burger's influence over the *majority opinion*—the document that states the Court's rationale for a decision. Majority opinions matter because they are an important source of *precedent*, meaning that they influence how similar cases will be decided in the future, both by the Supreme Court and by other federal courts. Thus, Burger's vote switching helped to maximize his influence over the Court's future decisions, even when he did not like the outcome preferred by a majority of his colleagues.

Making Decisions and Writing Opinions

The first step in understanding the strategic value of voting last is to consider how members of the Court make their decisions. Consider the example of *Texas v. Johnson*, a 1989 case that decided the constitutionality of a federal law that banned the burning of the American flag. (The law was struck down by a 5–4 vote.)

The first step in the Court's consideration of *Texas v. Johnson* was oral arguments, where proponents and opponents of the law make presentations to the justices. After oral arguments, justices began a process of individual reflection, consultation with colleagues, and further research. Ultimately, the chief justice scheduled the case for a meeting—called a *case conference*—where the law's fate would be decided.

The procedures used at the case conference are fairly simple. Cases are considered in order. When a case comes up, there is first some discussion where justices give their opinions. The justices speak in order of seniority, with the chief justice speaking first, followed by the associate justice who has been on the Court the longest, then the associate justice with the second-longest tenure, and so on.

Following discussion, the justices vote on the case using majority rule. Whichever option (uphold, strike down) receives a majority of votes wins—a tie means the law is upheld. The justices announce their votes in reverse order of seniority, with the chief justice voting last. By tradition, votes are supposed to be consistent with comments made during the discussion period. If, for example, a justice says that he thinks that a flag-burning law is unconstitutional, he is expected to vote to strike it down. Burger's "phony vote" strategy obviously violated this tradition.

After a case has been voted on, the next step is to assign one member of the Court to write the majority opinion. This document gives the rationale for the Court's decision—why a law was or was not constitutional. In the *Johnson* case, for example, the majority opinion explains why flag burning must be considered a form of speech, arguing that the government's interest in protecting a national symbol does not outweigh the rights of an individual to express her opinion by burning an American flag.

The majority opinion is an important document because the Court's decisions set precedents both for other federal courts and for the future Supreme Court. The opinion explains how the rules or principles used to resolve the current case will apply to other cases brought in the future. These principles are often expressed in the form of *tests*, lists of questions that can be used as a guide to future decisions by other courts.

An opinion can result in a narrow or wide foundation for precedence. In the case of *Texas v. Johnson*, for example, a majority opinion could have said that the circumstances of this case were very exceptional, implying that it's very easy to construct a flag burning law that doesn't violate the Constitution. In this opinion, the test might say, "Does the government have any other motive for this law besides preventing someone from expressing their opinion by burning a flag? If they do, the law is constitutional." This test would make it easier for the future Supreme Court and other federal courts to uphold (keep in place) any new flag burning laws that might be enacted.

At the other extreme, the majority opinion in *Texas v. Johnson* could state that flag burning is always a form of speech, so that it can't be banned except in very special circumstances. An example of such a test might ask, "In enacting this law, is the government trying to prevent a clear and immediate danger, such as burning a flag indoors where the flames might spread? If they are, than the law is constitutional, but if not, it should be struck down." This test would make it harder for future courts to uphold laws that banned flag burning.

As this discussion suggests, the content of a majority opinion is almost as important as the decision itself. Opinions can extend the impact of a decision over a range of future cases—or limit its impact to the particular case being decided. Opinions can also change how future cases are decided by offering different rationales or tests to lower courts. All in all, Supreme Court justices will be concerned with both the Court's decisions and with the content of opinions that explain these decisions.

The importance of the majority opinion suggests an obvious question: Who gets to write this document? Assignment is in the hands of one of two people. If the chief justice is in the majority, she decides who writes the opinion. If, however, the chief is not part of the majority, the most-senior associate justice in the majority controls the assignment, where seniority is defined in terms of time on the Court.

An example will help to illustrate the assignment process. Suppose that Congress has passed a law, the Internet Access Act of 2000, designed to increase the number of households that can connect to the Internet at high speeds and to insure that no Internet service provider can monopolize a local market. The act instructs the Federal Communications Commission (FCC) to develop new rules and regulations that balance the goal of getting more people on line with the goal of encouraging competition and preventing monopolies.

Fast-forward one year: Only a few additional homes have been wired, mainly because the FCC has decided to prohibit firms from offering high-speed access in an area unless they have at least one competitor. This rule prevents the formation of monopolies, but it also makes it impossible for a firm to do business in an area unless other firms enter at the same time. The firms take the FCC to court, arguing that the commission has misinterpreted their mandate from Congress and is engaging in an unconstitutional restraint of commerce. The case winds up before the Supreme Court, whose members must decide whether the FCC regulations are constitutional.

Suppose the Court has the same nine members as it did in fall 1999: Chief Justice Rehnquist and Associate Justices Breyer, Ginsberg, Kennedy, O'Connor, Scalia, Souter, Stevens, and Thomas.

If Rehnquist is in the majority when a case is voted on, he controls the assignment of the majority opinion. He can write it himself or give the job to any other member of the majority. Any member of the minority can write a *dissenting* opinion that gives their reasons for acting as they did. And members of the majority are free to write an additional *concurring* opinion in which they explain their behavior.

Why Vote Last. At first glance, the description of how the Court makes decisions only deepens the mystery of Burger's vote switching. Because justices are unelected, they have no reason to worry about how others, such as constituents, will evaluate their votes. Their sole concern should be with the outcome—the resolution of the case. Why, then, was Chief Justice Burger so intent on voting with the majority, even when he disagreed with their reasoning or their views on how the case should be decided?

Burger's action is even more puzzling because his vote switching had no effect on the outcome of the cases under consideration. For example, Justice Brennan's complaints about "phony votes" referred to Burger's behavior on an obscure Supreme Court case, *Thermtron Products, Inc. v. Hermansdorfer*. The essence of the case was whether a lower court had acted properly or improperly in its handling of a dispute between a company, Thermtron Products, and an individual, Hermansdorfer. Without Burger's vote, the eight remaining justices split as follows:

Majority (uphold lower court): White, Brennan, Marshall, Black-
mun, and Powell
Minority (reverse lower court ruling): Rehnquist, Stewart
Did not vote: Stevens

The important thing to realize is that, given these coalitions, Burger's vote had no impact on the outcome of the case. Without Burger, there were five votes to uphold the lower court and two votes to reverse it. If Burger voted with the majority, the result would be a 6–2 decision. If he voted with the minority, the result would have been a 5–3 decision. Either way, the case would be decided in favor of the lower court.

The discussion of this case in Woodward and Armstrong's book makes clear that Burger agreed with the minority (Rehnquist and Stewart) that the lower court had behaved improperly.[3] He had said as much during the case conference. Later in the conference, however, he argued that he really intended to vote with the majority and switched his vote after the other justices had announced their votes. Why?

The answer lies in the procedure used to assign opinions. If Burger votes with the majority, he gets to assign the majority opinion—that's because he's the chief justice. If he votes with the minority (which is what his preferences about the case tell him to do), the power to as-sign the opinion goes to the most senior associate justice in the ma-jority, in this case William Brennan. In general, Burger was more conservative than Brennan and might well be worried that Brennan would assign the opinion to himself or a like-minded colleague, re-sulting in an opinion that would not be to Burger's liking.

Once we consider control over opinion assignment, Burger's vote

---

[3]Woodward and Armstrong 1979, 418–19.

switching makes perfect sense. Burger's switch didn't change how the case was decided. However, it allowed Burger to maintain control over an important factor in the outcome—who writes the majority opinion and presumably the details of this opinion, which could critically narrow its ability to set precedent. Burger would likely assign the opinion to a member of the majority whose views were closest to his own. Or Burger would choose to write the opinion himself.

More Vote Switching: Abortion Rights. It is clear that other justices on the Supreme Court suspected that Burger's vote switches were precisely the kind of strategic behavior discussed here. William Douglas, for example, saw Burger's vote switching during the 1972 abortion cases (including the most famous abortion case, *Roe v. Wade*) as a clear example of Burger trying to manipulate the outcome[4], not of the vote but of the opinion.

Douglas wanted the Court to make a strong statement in favor of abortion rights by striking down the Texas law restricting abortion that was the focus of *Roe v. Wade* and by stating this right as a constitutional guarantee. Burger's exact position is unclear, but he certainly opposed Douglas's plan and may even have favored a decision that upheld the Texas law.

What did Burger do? Initially he stated his opposition to establishing a woman's right to have an abortion. Later, he argued that he had meant to vote the other way. Why the switch? For one thing, regardless of Burger's vote, a majority of the Court favored some sort of expanded abortion rights. Moreover, unless Burger voted with the majority, Douglas, who was the most senior associate justice in the majority, would assign the majority opinion. Douglas could write the opinion or give it to another justice who was sympathetic to his views.

In this situation, Burger had an obvious motive for behaving strategically. By switching to the majority, he wouldn't change the outcome of the case (the state abortion law would still be overturned), but he would get to control what the majority opinion said.

For example, Burger could have assigned the opinion to a member of the majority, such as Associate Justice Byron White, who favored overturning the law, but who also thought that state and federal governments should be allowed to regulate the availability of abortion throughout a woman's pregnancy. Such an opinion would have been

[4]For details on this example, see Woodward and Armstrong 1979, 171–73.

much more compatible with Burger's preferences than the one that was actually written, which struck down virtually all attempts to regulate abortions during the first trimester of pregnancy and allowed only some regulations thereafter.

The discussion in *The Brethren* suggests that Burger had two other motivations for switching. First, he might have wanted to delay assignment of the opinion so that it would not be released during an election year. (Burger was a supporter of then-President Nixon and might have wanted to help the president's reelection by putting off the release of a controversial decision.)

Another possibility is that Burger hoped to assign the opinion to a justice whose work would not gain the support of a majority on the Court. This result would lead to the case being reargued in 1973. At the time that Burger and Douglas were sparring over the opinion, there were two vacancies on the Court. Douglas feared that if the abortion cases were delayed, President Nixon would have time to appoint two antiabortion justices to the Court, transforming a proabortion majority into a majority that favored strong restrictions.

Ultimately, Burger and Douglas, arrived at a compromise: A third justice, Harry Blackmun, wrote the majority opinion on *Roe v. Wade* —an assignment that was closer to what Douglas wanted than what Burger preferred. Even so, the fact that Burger did not control this choice to the degree that he wanted to should not overshadow the fact that he tried very hard to do so.

Why didn't Burger just ignore Douglas and use his assignment power to control who wrote the opinion? Because, since it was obvious by then that Burger had switched his vote in an attempt to control the process, pressing through with an assignment that ignored Douglas's concerns would entail significant costs: Burger would receive no small measure of scorn from some of his colleagues on the Court, some might be less willing to work with Burger on future cases, and Burger's duplicity might have even led to changes in how opinions were assigned, reducing or eliminating the Chief Justice's power.

Vote Switching and Rationality

This section has investigated one example of strategic behavior on the Supreme Court: vote switching by the chief justice. This behavior is not irrational, stupid, or driven by a desire to be on the winning side. Rather, vote switching is a rational strategy that allows the chief justice to control an important feature of the Court's decisions, the selection of who writes the majority opinion.

While it is impossible to be sure, it is probably correct to assume that Chief Justice Burger's propensity for strategic behavior is the rule rather than the exception on the Supreme Court. Justices are not politicians, in the sense that they don't have to worry about re-election. But they have one important thing in common with elected officials: Their actions are driven by preferences, by their beliefs about what government should and should not be doing. To put it another way, justices don't lose their policy preferences when they put on their judicial black robes.

The Limits on Judicial Review

In the system of government laid out in the U.S. Constitution, the primary function of the Supreme Court is judicial review. The nine members of the Court have the power to declare laws and other government actions to be unconstitutional, or null and void. This section considers a fundamental question about this institution: What are the limits on judicial review?

At first glance, judicial review appears to contradict the idea of checks and balances that is supposed to be at the core of the U.S. Constitution. How can it be that no branch can impose policy on the others, if members of the Court can intervene at the end of the policy-making process and invalidate the work of the legislative and executive branches?

Scholars typically cite two limits on judicial review. The first limit is born of the fact that members of the Court must rely on other branches to implement their decisions. Justices may want to do truly outlandish things, but they refrain because they know that the president, members of Congress, and bureaucrats will not take the actions necessary to translate such decisions into law.

In the modern era, where compliance with judicial rulings is usually assumed, the idea that people would ignore a Supreme Court ruling may seem farfetched. But it is not. In the early 1800s, a Court headed by Chief Justice John Marshall held that the federal government had violated certain provisions in a treaty with the Cherokee Indians and ordered the government to change these policies imme-

diately. President Andrew Jackson did no such thing. In fact, legend
has it that upon hearing of the decision, he said, "John Marshall has
made his decision, now let him enforce it."

More recently, the Chief of Staff to President Nixon, Alexander
Haig, made a similar threat when justices were deciding whether to
force Nixon to give up tapes of oval office conversations—tapes that
later proved Nixon's participation in the Watergate cover-up.

The second argument for why judicial review is a limited power is
that justices are sensitive to their role in the American political system
and are careful to avoid going "too far." Suppose the members of the
Court think that the president and members of Congress enact many
laws that are of questionable value. Even under these circumstances,
they are unlikely to declare these laws unconstitutional simply because they don't like them. Indiscriminate judicial review might well
force members of Congress, the president, and state legislators to
change this institution—enact an amendment to the Constitution
that limits judicial review or abolishes it entirely.

An example of this attitude is seen in the majority opinion on
Chevron U.S.A. Inc. v. Natural Resources Defense Council, Inc. et. al.
The Chevron Corporation alleged that the Environmental Protection
Agency had misinterpreted some provisions of the 1977 Clean Air
Act. The majority of the Court held that an agency's interpretations
are binding, unless they contradict the plain wording of the statute.
In other words, justices usually give agencies the benefit of the
doubt; believing that the responsibility for implementation rests with
the agency, they are not going to get involved in cases where statutes
are vague or where an agency may have violated the spirit but not the
letter of a law.

Both of these explanations for the restrictions the Court imposes
on itself in the exercise of its power rely on the good will or insight of
justices. Neither addresses what would happen in the absence of this
good will and insight. Given that the writers of the Constitution imposed institutional checks or formal limits on the powers of other
branches of government, it doesn't make sense that they would leave
members of the Court unconstrained.

In this section, you will see that the rules governing the Court's
review power embody strong limits on how this power can be used.[5]

---

[5]This argument is taken from William N. Eskridge and John Ferejohn, "Making the
Deal Stick: Enforcing the Original Constitutional Structure in the Modern Regulatory State," *Journal of Law, Economics, and Organization* 8.1 (1992): 165–87.

That is, judicial review is not an institution that confers unlimited power. Justices cannot rule on whatever laws they wish. Nor can they impose a new outcome after finding that a law is unconstitutional. These institutional limits on judicial review serve to mitigate or even eliminate the danger that members of the Court will misuse their review power.

What Is Judicial Review?

Judicial review occurs when the members of the Supreme Court consider whether a law or other government action is consistent with the powers and limits set out in the Constitution. Laws or actions that a majority finds to be consistent are said to be *constitutional* and allowed to remain in place. However, a majority can also decide that a law or action is *unconstitutional*, in which case it becomes null and void.

At first glance, judicial review appears to violate an essential element of the checks and balances that our Constitution is supposed to embody. The essence of checks and balances is that the members of one branch of government or legislative chamber cannot impose policy outcomes on everyone else. For example, the House of Representatives cannot pass a law without the Senate's consent and the president's signature (or an override). But can checks and balances exist if Supreme Court justices are free to determine what's constitutional? What happens if a group of judges decide to review laws based on their own policy preferences, rather than focusing on what the Constitution allows and does not allow?

Recall my previous example of the Internet Access Act of 2000—a hypothetical law that instructs the FCC to develop new rules and regulations for high-speed Internet access. Based on the act, the FCC has decided to prohibit firms from offering high-speed access in an area unless they have at least one competitor. This rule prevents the formation of monopolies, but it also makes it impossible for a firm to do business in an area unless other firms enter at the same time. The firms take the FCC to court, arguing that the FCC has misinterpreted Congress's mandate and are engaging in an unconstitutional restraint of commerce.

Now suppose all nine justices on the Court in 2000 are confirmed web surfers. They subscribe to America Online, trade stocks on line at E*Trade, buy all their books, videos, and software at Amazon.com, and bid on eBay auctions for rare Beanie Babies. Because of these interests, the justices favor a different set of Internet regulations, changing the two-provider rule to allow some exceptions or abandoning it entirely. The question is: Can the justices get what they want using judicial review?

The Court's Jurisdiction. In general, the Constitution gives the Supreme Court *appellate jurisdiction* over the cases it considers.[6] Appellate jurisdiction means that members of the Court hear cases on appeal, after they have first been adjudicated at a lower level of the federal court system (District Court or the Court of Appeals) or in state courts.

The impact of jurisdiction on the Court's powers is so obvious that it's hard to see. Simply put, the nine justices are unable to rule on a case unless one of the parties involved is unhappy with a lower-court ruling and is willing to bear the time and costs associated with an appeal to the Supreme Court. Justices cannot reach down to a lower court and grab an interesting case. They have to wait for the case to come to them.

Because the Supreme Court has appellate jurisdiction, situations can easily arise where the justices will be unable to use their judicial review powers, even when they want to. People who are upset by a governmental action may not take an agency or Congress to court in the first place. And if they get something close enough to what they want from a lower court or lose their enthusiasm for judicial proceedings, the justices of the Supreme Court will never get to rule on their case.

Consider how appellate jurisdiction would complicate review of the Internet Access Act. The justices want to change the FCC's rules to increase high-speed access to the Internet. The problem is, they can review the FCC's rulings only if someone challenges the rules in court, isn't satisfied with a lower-court ruling, and persists through all of the steps needed for Court consideration. If the plaintiffs lose interest at any point or are able to compromise with the FCC, the justices will find themselves in the position of having the power to overturn the FCC's regulations but being unable to exercise this power in the first place.

---

[6]The only exceptions, where the Court has original jurisdiction, are cases involving Indian treaties, controversies involving two or more states, cases brought by one state against the citizens of another state, and cases involving foreign ambassadors.

Reversion Point. The second thing to understand about judicial review is that it doesn't give justices complete freedom to make policy. Rather, if justices find that a law or regulation is unconstitutional, government policy will revert to one of two outcomes: the policy originally intended by Congress or whatever policy was in place before the law was enacted.

For example, with regard to the Internet Access Act, if the case does reach the Court, the members of the Court have three options. First, they can uphold the FCC's regulations. Upholding a law or regulation means that it remains in place. If, for example, a majority on the Court upholds the Internet Access Act and the FCC's interpretation of what it says, then the FCC's new rules will continue in force without change.

Second, members of the Court can strike down the Internet Access Act—declare that it is unconstitutional. If they do, then policy reverts back to whatever policy existed before the law was passed. Thus, if the Court struck down the Internet Access Act entirely, the FCC's new rules would be invalid, and Internet service providers would be regulated by whatever rules were in place before passage of the Act.

Finally, the justices can decide that the act is constitutional but that the FCC commissioners misinterpreted what they were supposed to do. This option is particularly appealing given the preferences of Court members in this example. All nine justices like the goals of the Internet Access Act (high-speed web surfing for all), but they don't like how the FCC has implemented this policy (by guarding against monopolies, the agency has slowed the move to high-speed access).

What happens after a Court majority strikes down an agency action? The effect is to turn back the clock and force agency bureaucrats to develop a new set of regulations. In other words, the members of the Court tell the agency: "You didn't do what the Congress and the president told you to do. Read the statute again, start from scratch, and make new rules."

These three options identify the limits on judicial review. Simply put, the fact that the Supreme Court has the power of judicial review does not mean that a majority of justices can impose whatever policy outcomes they prefer. They can direct the FCC to make new rules, for instance, but they cannot write the rules themselves.

Faced with a law or agency ruling to review, the justices have a very limited range of options. They can uphold the law or ruling, which preserves whatever policy is in place. They can strike down the law, which restores whatever policy existed before the law was passed. Or they can strike down an agency's interpretation of the law, forcing the agency to adopt new rules reflecting Congress's intent.

This narrow set of options means that a would-be renegade Court has little room to impose its preferences on the other branches of government. In the case of the Internet Access Act, the justices might want rules that mandate the installation of high-speed lines throughout the country, starting in the neighborhoods where they live. But judicial review does not give this power to members of the Court. They can approve of the FCC's interpretation, instruct the agency to move its regulations closer to the intent of the law, or move policy back to what existed before the law was passed. Their power to impose outcomes is limited to these three options.

Finally, the policy-making process need not end with the Court's decision. Suppose that a majority on the Court decides that the Internet Access Act is unconstitutional, meaning that the FCC's regulations revert to whatever they looked like before passage of the act. Certainly this decision is the last word for the Internet Act—remember, "from this Court there is no appeal." However, even after a united Court renders its decision, there is nothing to stop members of Congress from passing a new version of the Internet Access Act that achieves the same ends by constitutional means or passing a different law that creates a new outcome. The justices can overturn these laws as well but all that does is preserve the status quo. The justices can prevent Congress from enacting new policies that they don't like, but they cannot use judicial review to shift policy to a new outcome that they alone prefer.

Judicial Review: A Summary

Members of the Supreme Court exercise the power of judicial review. However, this institution does not make them truly supreme. Supreme Court justices must wait for cases to come to them. Moreover, even if they abandon any pretense of making objective judgments on the constitutionality of laws and statutes, they have a very limited range of choices and cannot use judicial review to impose their preferences on the rest of the country.

In sum, there is no need to worry that members of the Supreme Court will decide one day to misuse judicial review, substituting their own views for the policies enacted by members of Congress and the president. The reason is not that Supreme Court justices are nice people, that they are worried that their decisions will be ignored, or that they are unaware of how powerful they truly are. Rather, they can't misuse judicial review because of limitations contained in the institutions that set out the jurisdiction of the Supreme Court and that determine what happens after this power is used.

Summary

Members of the Supreme Court are rational actors with policy preferences, just like elected officials and unelected bureaucrats. The fact that they behave strategically is seen in Burger's vote switching as well as in both the conventional wisdom about judicial review and the interpretation developed here. That they hold policy preferences is seen in the discussion of any Court decision.

Some readers may be distressed by the idea that members of the Court are no better than politicians, in that they have policy preferences that they work to implement. But as we see in the case of judicial review, these preferences are sometimes very useful. They give members of the Court a reason to consider cases that involve an agency's interpretation of a statue as well as a reason to overturn agency actions that are a departure from what Congress intended. They also force justices to consider how their decisions will affect public policy and the welfare of citizens throughout the nation. And institutional rules prevent them from imposing their preferences even in the absence of these considerations.

9

Conclusion

At the start of this book, I claimed that focusing on individual rationality and political institutions would provide deep insight into the workings of American politics. Here I'm going to return to these themes as a way of summarizing the central findings of this book.

Perhaps the most important lesson you should take from this book is an understanding of its limitations. To begin with, these chapters are only an introduction to American politics and to rational choice. Many institutions and behaviors have not been mentioned much less explained.

Moreover, it would be a mistake to take these explanations of politics in America and apply them willy-nilly to the rest of the world. Some concepts will generalize: the ideas that people are rational, that institutions are important, and that information is valuable. However, voters and politicians in other countries sometimes have very different goals than the ones described here and operate within a radically different set of rules and institutions. These differences need to be understood in order to make sense of politics in other nations.

You must also keep in mind that this book is only an introduction to rational-choice theory and its application to American politics. My philosophy has been to keep things simple, substituting words and examples for formulas and complex derivations. I hope that you are interested enough to keep learning about rational choice, but in any case you should remember that the conclusions developed here are by no means the last word on any of the topics.

Finally, it would be a mistake for you to conclude that rational-choice theory is the only valid approach to studying politics. Many scholars rely on assumptions drawn from other fields—such as social psychology—assumptions that specify very different pictures of how people go about making choices. In addition, some questions, such as those involving fairness and justice, are impossible to answer with a focus on prediction and explanation. And finally, some scholars avoid trying to explain American politics, instead offering valuable and insightful descriptions.

Obviously, I think that rational-choice assumptions provide considerable insight into how American politics works. Otherwise why write this book? But I don't want you to become a rational-choice robot who can't look at politics any other way. American politics is studied using many different approaches. My advice is to do the same.

Rational People, Rational Choices

This book has drawn a picture of American politics in which the participants—voters, politicians, interest-group representatives, and judges—are rational, if sometimes not very smart. Their actions are driven by goals and expectations about the likely behavior of others and shaped by uncertainty about many relevant factors.

Take voters. By now you should be comfortable with the assumption that voters have preferences and that these preferences drive their political participation. However, this rationality must be set in context. The average voter knows little about how policies are made or the fine points of legislative strategy. He is often ignorant about candidates' platforms as well as the details of policy proposals. And many voters rely on informational shortcuts, such as judging candidates by their race, their gender—or even their ability to eat tamales.

Is the average voter's persistent, pervasive ignorance a sign of irrationality? No. On the contrary, this voter is the epitome of a rational actor. Her detachment from politics makes sense given the high costs of learning and the small benefits from doing so. Shortcuts are used because they minimize the cost of participation. You might wish that voters were more involved in the political process, but you cannot say that they are making a dumb choice in light of their interests and constraints.

What do these examples imply? If you are trying to make sense of American politics, you should begin with the idea that the participants know what they are doing. Many of the chapters here show how seemingly random, clueless, or downright stupid behavior has a sensible, even intelligent explanation. Thus, if you find examples of seemingly bizarre, irrational political behavior, your initial premise should be that an explanation lies in the motives or the beliefs of the participants or in the institutions that shape their interactions, not in an inability to make good choices.

Individuals Shape Outcomes

This book has explained politics one participant at a time. With this perspective comes the assumption that things don't happen by accident. Laws aren't made because "the government" acts. Rather, all of the phenomena described here—from vote decisions to judicial decisions, from collective action to pork-barrel politics—can be traced back to the actions of real people making rational choices.

The notion that politics is best understood in terms of individual actions implies that government is not fundamentally out of control. Anything government does—a new law, an agency ruling, or a judicial decision—is the product of actual decisions by real people. You can always find someone to blame or someone to congratulate. And you should look to the participants, their motives, and their information, in order to understand how an outcome came to be.

It is important to think of participation as a variable. It's just as rational to get involved as it is to abstain. However, if you're thinking of opting out entirely, remember that abstention doesn't stop the political process. It may express your preference for the status quo, but it does not guarantee that this outcome will be sustained. The only thing abstention guarantees is that someone else will make choices, someone who may not be inclined to take your preferences into account.

The Role of Political Institutions

Institutions matter. This premise has been demonstrated throughout the book. Collective action is made easier by institutions that make coercion possible, provide selective incentives, or allow people to monitor the behavior of others. Primary elections lead candidates to move their platforms away from the media voter and toward primary electorates. And laws such as the Administrative Procedures Act or the Freedom of Information Act help make fire-alarm oversight possible.

These examples also illustrate the principle that institutions are never neutral. Different institutions often produce different outcomes. For example, taking away the president's veto power is likely to change the content of many laws passed by members of Congress. Deciding how to decide is not a dry, unimportant prelude to the real debate over outcomes. Rather, choices involving institutions have a direct and immediate impact on the result of group decisions.

These results also imply that, in politics and elsewhere, knowledge of the rules confers an enormous amount of power. People who pay attention to the rules and who learn what their colleagues want do better than people who are indifferent to these factors. Put another way, people who see politics as a grand battle of ideas and principles will generally lose to opponents who see it as a process to be understood and won.

A related lesson is that you cannot think of institutions in abstract terms—"Is this a good rule?" Rather, you should think like a politician. Politicians don't worry about whether an institution is good or bad. Rather, they try to figure out where the institution will take them and whether they like where they're going. The way to think about rules is in terms of what you want.

Evaluating American Politics and American Government

Many people have trouble accepting the idea that bad things can happen in a rational world. When they hear about the failure of government policies, widespread voter ignorance and abstention, the enactment of wasteful pork-barrel proposals, campaigns where candidates fail to talk about the issues, or many similar events, they find it hard to believe that the political process works well or to accept a view of politics that is based on the assumption of rational choice.

If people are rational, why do bad things happen? One reason is that people know what they want but not how to get it. For example, legislators often must deal with complex, intractable public problems to which there are no obvious solutions. In the aftermath of the shootings at Columbine High School in Littleton, Colorado, members of Congress considered how to prevent teen violence. What is the answer—better gun-control laws, more parental attention, instruction in morality and personal responsibility, or what? The only true answer is that no one knows.

Given the complexity of problems that politicians and bureaucrats are given to solve, it is no surprise that their efforts to solve them often fall short. The difficulty is not a lack of will, time, or rationality. Rather, the problem is a lack of solutions and no idea about how to develop them.

A second explanation for the failure of rationality to provide good outcomes is that even when information is available, rational actors may choose to live with their uncertainty and with the possibility of mistakes. Chapter Six noted that many voters overestimate the benefits and underestimate the costs of pork-barrel proposals. Should you fault these voters for failing to invest the time needed to understand distributive proposals fully? No. Unless the voter is a political junkie, such information is of little value. The average voter's demand for more and more distributive benefits is rational behavior, despite the fact that it can provoke elected officials to build bridges where there are no rivers.

A similar lesson can be drawn from the average voter's reliance on shortcuts and other rules of thumb. Chapter Four showed that many votes are based on race, gender, and other nonpolitical factors. While these shortcuts minimize the costs of voting, they create the possibility of mistakes. A candidate who enjoys a plate of tamales may have no sympathy for the interests of Mexican-American voters. Yet because these shortcuts lower the costs of voting, it is no surprise that rational voters choose to rely on them.

A third explanation for why rational behavior might produce bad outcomes comes from the discussion of collective action in Chapter Three. As you saw, the fact that a group of people can make themselves better off by working together does not guarantee that they will organize to do so. This unhappy result can occur even when everyone in the group knows that cooperation is beneficial and when people are free to communicate their good intentions. Rationality at the individual level does not always result in optimal results for the members of a group.

Finally, the fact that a person is rational does not imply that his actions are good for everyone. Consider pork-barrel politics. Legislators pursue reelection by enacting proposals that send benefits to their districts. But the increased taxes voters pay to fund these proposals often exceed the benefits they receive. Does the fact that pork-barrel bills are enacted mean that legislators are irrational? No. It only means that they are willing to impose costs on others in order to achieve their goals.

The fact that politics is a lot more rational that most people think is both good news and bad news. On the one hand, saying that things are rational means that they are explainable. It's important to know that people who refuse to join interest groups aren't just clueless or that they fail to see the gains possible from successful collective action. The problem lies with their incentives not an inability to see the consequences of their choices.

The bad news about saying people are rational is that it suggests there are no easy solutions. Collective-action problems are intractable precisely because they result from rational calculation. Suppose you found a group of people who weren't cooperating and carefully explained to them the benefits of doing so. Would this information change their behavior? Probably not, unless you also created mechanisms to provide selective incentives to cooperators or gave someone the power to coerce cooperation. The problem is not that the people are making bad choices; rather, it's that rational action leads them to a bad outcome.

In the end, the problem lies in our standards. Most Americans want perfection from democracy and from government. This expectation ignores reality. Politics is fundamentally a messy, complex enterprise. The solution is not to waste time complaining or to abandon all hope. The solution is to understand how politics works both to develop a better set of standards and to pursue your own interests within the process.

Index